I0032792

A Short
Historical Introduction
to
The Law
of
Real Property

A Short
Historical Introduction
to
The Law
of
Real Property

By

J. John Lawler
University of Pittsburgh School of Law

and

Gail Gates Lawler
of the Philadelphia Bar

BeardBooks
Washington, D.C.

Copyright 1940 by J.John Lawler and Gail Gates Lawler

Reprinted 2000 by Beard Books, Washington, D.C.

ISBN 1-58798-032-0

Printed in the United States of America

To Our Parents

PREFACE

An introductory course in Real Property must lay a sound foundation for further work in that field. A student in his first year of legal study makes his acquaintance with several fields, e.g., Contracts, Torts, Agency, Crimes, where the terminology and the factual situations lie within the ambit of his personal experience or general knowledge. Consequently, his greatest interest tends to center on one of those fields. In Real Property he comes in contact with factual relationships entirely outside his experience or general knowledge, and they are further obscured by a terminology which is completely new to him.

Real Property Law can be understood only in the light of its historical evolution. "Let me speak first of those fields where there can be no progress without history. I think the law of real property supplies the readiest example. No lawgiver, meditating a code of laws conceived the system of feudal tenures. History built up the system and the law that went with it. Never by the process of logical deduction from the idea of abstract ownership could we distinguish the incidents of an estate in fee simple from those of an estate for life, or those of an estate for life from those of an estate for years. Upon these points 'a page of history is worth a volume of logic'" (Holmes in N. Y. Trust Co. v. Eisner, May 16, 1921, 256 U.S. 345, 41 S. Ct. 506, 65 L. Ed. 963, 16 A.L.R. 660). "So it is wherever we turn in the forest of the law of land. Restraints upon alienations, the suspension of absolute ownership, contingent remainders, executory devises, private trusts and trusts for charities, all these heads of the law are intelligible only in the light of history, and get from history the impetus which must shape their subsequent development" (Cardozo, Nature of the Judicial Process, 1921, p. 54).

The "Cases and Materials" type of presentation was developed in an attempt to meet this need. Unfortunately, however, since the "Materials" usually consist of a long series of quotations lifted bodily from the contexts which made them comprehensible, written in the varying styles and languages of six centuries, they have a tendency to confuse and annoy rather than to aid. The beginning student in Real Property who can read successive excerpts from Bracton, Littleton, Coke, Leake, Blackstone, and Williams dealing with an identical problem and derive therefrom any historical benefit is rare. In addition, the American material has been examined in a scanty fashion. Some phases of the subject have not been touched. Other phases have received excellent treatment from such extremely able property scholars as Kales, Vance, Bordwell, Powell, and a few others, but unfortunately this material is scattered in legal periodicals. The student can be referred, of course, to those works in their original form, but the material is widely scattered within those works, and not every Law School Library is in a position to furnish the material in sufficient quantity to enable a first year class to use it advantageously.

This short book is an attempt to meet that need. There was practically no original research in its preparation. It is little more than a paraphrase within a single short volume of material which has already been worked and presented by profound scholars of legal history such as Holdsworth, Digby, Pollock and Maitland, Bordwell, Vance, Kales, and Powell. Any virtue which does pertain to this book lies in that it makes this material accessible (and we hope easily comprehensible) to first year students in Real Property. For obvious reasons, then, there is no attempt to cite sources in exhaustive footnotes. A student who wishes to investigate any particular topic further will be led to the most important sources by the bibliography which follows each chapter.

The arrangement may seem a trifle unconventional. In the customary presentation each incident, such as creation, alienation, devisability, is presented as a unit, in what might be termed a horizontal method. In each incident its operation with reference to various types of interests is examined. This frequently results in a surprising number of lacunae in otherwise well done books. In stating conveyancing as a separate subject matter, for example, there is a tendency to overemphasize certain types of conveyances and certain relations to the detriment of others. Our method might be termed a vertical method in contradistinction to the customary presentation. Each interest has been presented as a unit and examined with reference to the various incidents. We feel that by this method we have achieved two objectives: first, it was possible to avoid lacunae; second, any questions which arise in the student's mind with reference to a particular type of interest can be answered by reading the material in one place—under that type of interest, instead of searching through the material on each incident separately.

If this work aids first year students in grasping the essentials of their introduction to the intricacies of the Law of Real Property, we shall feel well satisfied.

J. JOHN LAWLER
GAIL GATES LAWLER

Pittsburgh, Pa.

TABLE OF CONTENTS

CHAPTER I

THE METHOD OF HOLDING LAND—FEUDAL TENURES

ix

TABLE OF CONTENTS

C. FREE AND COMMON SOCAGE

TABLE OF CONTENTS

CHAPTER II

ESTATES IN LAND

A. ESTATES OF PRESENT ENJOYMENT

I. Freehold Estates

a. Fee Simple

b. Qualified Fee Simple

c. Maritagium

TABLE OF CONTENTS

d. Conditional Fee

e. Fee Tail

f. Life Estates

xiii

II. Non-Freehold Estates—Varieties

a. Term for Years

TABLE OF CONTENTS

b. Tenancy at Will

c. Tenancy from Year to Year—Periodic Tenancy

d. Tenancy at Sufferance

e. Non-Freehold Interests—Devolution on Death

f. Rent in Non-Freehold Interests

B. EXPECTANT ESTATES, OR PRESENT ESTATES OF FUTURE ENJOYMENT

I. Interests Arising Prior to the Statute of Uses

TABLE OF CONTENTS

a. Right of Re-entry for Condition Broken (Power of Termination)

TABLE OF CONTENTS

d. Remainders

TABLE OF CONTENTS

TABLE OF CONTENTS

CHAPTER III

SEISIN, THE REAL ACTIONS AND ADVERSE POSSESSION

Table of Contents

Chapter IV

Incorporeal Interests

A. INCORPOREAL HEREDITAMENTS IMPORTANT ONLY AT COMMON LAW

TABLE OF CONTENTS

CHAPTER V

ESTATES HELD IN CO-OWNERSHIP

TABLE OF CONTENTS

CHAPTER I

THE METHOD OF HOLDING LAND—
FEUDAL TENURES

Section 1. Land Law Prior to the Norman Conquest.
The land law of England, which is the background of the land
law of the United States, has evolved from many different
systems. There is comparatively little definite knowledge of
the methods of holding land which prevailed prior to the
Norman Conquest of 1066. It seems that a large portion of
the land which was unoccupied was considered as being *"terra
regis,"* land out of which the king was accustomed to make
grants. The recipients of these grants had an alodial or
absolute ownership, but the king appears to have exercised
a certain sovereignty over all the land in the kingdom, and
the conferring of duties, privileges and jurisdiction was so
inextricably intermingled with the grant of the land that it
is impossible to determine how much of this is land law, how
much taxation or administration and how much procedure.

Below the king there seem to have been various types
of interests in the land and various methods of holding those
interests—accretions from the varying cultures to which ten
centuries of invasion had exposed the country. Very little of
the land law as it existed prior to the Conquest is significant
for our purposes. In those few instances, where it is, the
earlier law will be mentioned, but for purposes of the history
of the land law in general, a convenient point of departure is
found in the Norman Conquest.

1

Sec. 2. Norman Feudalism. In the eleventh century, there was, on the Continent, a highly developed political organization which had its roots in the land. Some vestigial remnants of the Roman law had survived the collapse of Roman rule, and out of these remnants and the necessities of the troubled times the feudal system had arisen.

The organization consisted primarily of a series of military alliances between neighboring chieftains, culminating in the ruler of the particular country. Each petty leader organized his own domain on the same lines as the kingdom, so that each leader's domain and the organization thereof was a replica of the principal organization, the feudal state. The neighborhood chieftain organized his military force and provided for the maintenance of the agricultural economy by which he lived by parcelling out portions of land to his followers in return for their services. Land thus held was spoken of as a "beneficium." The important part of the relationship between the leader and his followers was not the relationship of the parties to the land but the personal relationship of lord and man.

In addition, neighboring owners of small tracts of land who needed the protection of a powerful lord, surrendered their land to him and then received it back again from him. By the surrender and regrant of the land, which was called "commendation," the personal relationship of lord and man was created, which entitled the landholder to the lord's protection and entitled the lord to the landholder's allegiance and services. The lord himself had originally received his land from the ruler of the country in the creation of a personal relationship, importing, in the same way, protection on the one hand, and service on the other. It was a highly developed and efficient organization although it had a few obvious defects resulting from its extreme decentralization.

Under the rules of international law, a conqueror acquires sovereignty over the conquered land, but the ownership of the individual landowner who has not resisted him is not disturbed. When William the Conqueror defeated Harold at Hastings in 1066, he thereby acquired title to all the land which had been owned by Harold himself, and also all that had been owned by those great men who had fought on Harold's side. It was only natural that the Norman William should apply to this land the system that had been developed in Normandy, with a few minor variations to avoid the known defects.

Sec. 3. Effect of the Norman Conquest on Land Holding in England. William at once proceeded to parcel out portions of the conquered territory to his followers, thereby bringing a very considerable part of the realm immediately under the feudal system. Moreover, the need for protection by the nobles who had not actually supported Harold and by the rank and file whose landholdings had not been disturbed by the Conquest led them to transfer their lands to William or to one of William's followers, and receive them back again, thus raising the reciprocal obligations of lord and man. As a result of this process within a short time all of the land in England had been effectively placed under the feudal system.

In adapting the feudal system of Normandy to England, William made one notable change. In Continental feudalism the obligation of military service had run only to the immediate lord. This had been the most obvious defect since it made the levying of an effective military force very difficult. In Anglo-Saxon England there had been a certain type of military obligation running from every landholder to the king. William, conscious of the need of a strong central power, adapted the Anglo-Saxon idea to feudal tenure and henceforth the military obligation ran, not to the immediate lord, but to the king.

The man who received land from a lord was spoken of as the "holder" or "tenant" of the land. The land itself was called a "tenement" and the type of services the tenant was obliged to perform in return for the land he held distinguished the "tenure" in which the land was held. The three words "tenant," "tenement," and "tenure" all came from the Latin word *"tenere,"* meaning to hold; consequently even in using a purely Anglo-Saxon word we use the cognate "holder."

Sec. 4. Classes of Tenants. Those tenants who held their land directly of the king were called his tenants *in capite,* or chief tenants, while those who held their land of the tenants *in capite* were known as *mesne* tenants. The tenants who held their land of the *mesne* tenants were spoken of as tenants *paravail,* being those persons who were supposed to make "avail" or profit of the land. It will readily be seen that in this system only the highest in the scale, the king, and the lowest, the tenant *paravail,* occupied but a single position. The king, styled lord paramount, alone was always lord, never tenant; the tenant *paravail* alone was always tenant, never lord. All of the intervening parties were simultaneously tenant to those of whom they held their land, and lord to those who held land of them. Several persons thus held the particular tracts of land actually occupied by the tenant *paravail.* The one who possessed the land was said to be "seised in *demesne";* all those above him were said to be "seised in service."

Sec. 5. Types of Tenures. There were four types of free tenure by which lands were held: tenure by knight service, tenure in free and common socage, tenure in serjeanty and tenure in frankalmoign. The free tenures were those that were considered worthy of a free man. There was another type of tenure called unfree, tenure in villeinage.

A. KNIGHT SERVICE

Sec. 6. Tenure by Knight Service. Obviously, at the time of the Conquest, the services that would be of the greatest importance to the king, and in return for which he would be most likely to bestow land upon his followers, were of a military nature. Thus it was that, on the establishment of feudalism in England, tenure by knight service was the important type of tenure, and the method of tenure by which the great lords held their lands of the king. The great lords themselves who were in need of military services, also granted portions of their lands to be held of them by knight service. The tenure was initiated by the performance of the ceremony of homage, which was inseparable from its creation, since it was through the performance of that solemn ceremony that the essential personal relationship of lord and man came into existence. Bracton's [1] account of the ceremony was as follows: The tenant placed his hands between the hands of the lord in token of subjection to the lord, and said: "I become your man of the tenement that I hold of you and faith to you will bear of life and member and earthly worship (or, as some say, of body and chattels and earthly worship), and faith to you shall bear against all folk (some add, who can live and die) saving the faith that I owe to our lord the king." According to Britton,[2] the lord then kissed the tenant, and Littleton [3] added that the lord sat, while the tenant knelt, ungirt and with head uncovered. The tenant invariably swore an oath of fealty to the lord. Standing, with his hand placed on the gospels, he said,[4] "Hear this my lord, I will bear faith to you of life and member, goods, chattels and earthly worship, so help me God and these holy gospels of God."

The service required of the tenant who held his land by knight service was to provide a certain number of fully armed and equipped knights to do service in the king's wars. This service was owed for a limited period of time, usually stated to be forty days. Although it was apparently by no means unusual for the service to extend beyond that period, it would seem that, after the first forty days, wages were due. The number of knights to be supplied by the tenant varied in accordance with the amount of land held by him. The term "knight's fee" involved no particular acreage; it was simply the amount of land that was to supply one knight, and its extent varied.

---

[1] Bracton, f. 80. [2] II Britton, * 37.
[3] Littleton, sec. 85.
[4] Bracton, f. 80.

Although tenure by knight service is normally spoken of in connection with the tenant *in capite,* it must be remembered that the obligation of the tenant *in capite* was to provide as many knights as he held knight's fees. To obtain such knights who were to serve with him in satisfaction of his obligation to the king, the tenant *in capite* might in turn make grants of land to be held of him by knight service. All holdings by knight service were by no means restricted to the tenant *in capite.*

Sec. 7. **Transmutation of Military Service into Scutage.** The typical feudal tenure, tenure by knight service, flourished during the twelfth century. In its pure form that tenure lasted roughly only for the hundred years from 1066 to 1166. Just as the reasons for its growth are obvious, so too are the reasons for its decline. In time, the king, through his efforts to increase the royal power at the expense of the great lords, inevitably came into conflict with them. Under such circumstances, where the king's problem was that of coping with rebellious barons, a mercenary army was better adapted to his needs. Moreover, in foreign wars, the king found a mercenary army more useful. Before the end of the twelfth century the point had been reached where, at times, the king found it to his advantage to accept a money payment, known as *scutage* or *escuage,* in lieu of military service. In the century running roughly from 1166 to 1266 the kings employed professional soldiers, paying their wages from the scutage received. It must be kept in mind, however, that the levying of scutage was only occasional; in all history, such a payment does not seem to have been demanded more than forty times. An option of paying the scutage or furnishing the knights was not extended to the tenant *in capite.* In the thirteenth century the rate at which scutage was to be imposed was not determined until after the expiration of the campaign. During the reigns of Henry III and Edward I the tenant *in capite* who had disobeyed the call to military service had to pay far more than the scutage in the shape of a heavy fine for his disobedience. From the first, however, it seems that the king, when it was to his advantage to do so, was accustomed to collect scutage from the actual "tenant in *demesne*" who held his land by knight service; the king, at such times, dealt directly with the undertenant. Such tenants were in time able to establish the principle, that if they did not choose to serve in person, they could, instead, pay scutage. Tenure by knight service of a *mesne* lord had really become tenure by scutage or escuage rather than actual tenure by knight service.

The royal right to take scutage was limited by Magna Carta (1215), and in the fourteenth century Parliament claimed to exercise control over scutage. Scutage ceases to be of importance after the thirteenth century. Richard II remitted it in 1385. From the thirteenth century, tenure by knight service became merely a form of landholding.

Sec. 8. Incidents of Tenure by Knight Service—Homage and Fealty. In addition to the obligation of military service which was fixed in the grant, there were certain rights and privileges possessed by the lord which arose by operation of law and were called the incidents of tenure by knight service. We have already mentioned two of these incidents, homage and fealty. It may be added that the breach of the obligation involved in homage constituted a most serious offense in feudal times, being spoken of as a "felony."

Sec. 9. Incidents of Tenure by Knight Service—Relief— Rise of Inheritability of Lands. The relief was an important incident of tenure by knight service, since it was of value to the lord in augmenting his income. Originally, land held by knight service had not been inheritable. The land had been granted by that tenure to secure the services of an able warrior. There was no assurance that the warrior's heir would inherit his ancestor's qualities. It was only in the event that the heir measured up to the requisite standard of valor that it would be desirable to grant the land to him anew. If he did not possess the necessary qualifications, another, more worthy, from the lord's pragmatic standpoint, might better be given the land. By the middle of the thirteenth century, however, when the services of professional mercenaries had replaced those of the knights themselves, that reason had lost its cogency, and it was considered that the heir of the holder had a right to succeed to the tenement on the tenant's death, but that he must pay for the privilege of becoming tenant in his ancestor's place. The relief was the payment for this privilege. The heir was, of course, also required to take an oath of fealty and do homage to the lord, thus becoming the lord's man and succeeding to the property. The admission by the lord of the heir as tenant was a favor that was to be purchased by the heir, but it was a favor that could not be withheld upon the payment of the requisite sum. Originally the amount seems to have been fixed by bargaining, but in the early part of the thirteenth century it was settled that the amount of the relief of a knight's fee was one hundred shillings.

Sec. 10.   **Incidents of Tenure by Knight Service—Primer Seisin.** The incident of *primer seisin* applied only to lands held directly of the king. When a tenant *in capite* died, the preliminaries to the payment of the relief differed from those where the land had been held of a *mesne* lord, the king being entitled to what was called *primer seisin*. Upon the death of the tenant *in capite* the king's escheator immediately took possession of the land, and proceeded to determine by inquest who was the rightful heir of the deceased. The right of the heir had to be established by the inquest before he was put into possession, and then he was given possession only after he had done homage and had either paid the relief, or had given security for its payment. Blackstone states [5] that the king was entitled to enter and receive the whole profits of the land, until livery was sued, and since that suit was commonly not made within a shorter time than a year and a day of the death of the tenant, the king as an average received the first year's fruits, or one year's profits of the land.

---

[5] II Blackstone, * 66-67.

Sec. 11. Incidents of Tenure by Knight Service—Wardship. Wardship was another incident of tenure by knight service that was of great practical importance, since it was a fruitful source of revenue to the lords. Where the tenant died leaving a minor heir or heiress, the lord had the right to become the minor's guardian. In the case of a minor heir, the guardianship lasted until he reached the age of 21; in the case of a minor heiress, the guardianship seems to have ended upon her reaching the age of 14, although that is a moot point. The duties of the guardian were only to see that the debts of the deceased were paid and that the minor was properly maintained and educated. All revenue beyond that required for those purposes became the property of the guardian, not in the character of a fiduciary, but in his own right. Since the excess revenue belonged to him outright, the guardian was not required to render an accounting of that revenue. Naturally this right was highly regarded and became a marketable commodity. It should be added that the guardian was not allowed to abuse or misuse the land, under penalty of forfeiting his wardship. The heir, on attaining his majority, had to purchase the livery of the lands by payment of a fine or half a year's profits of the lands. This was called livery or *"ousterlemain."*

If the deceased had held several different tenements from different *mesne* lords, each lord was entitled to the wardship of the tenement held of him. As to the wardship of the person of the heir, the lord of whom the deceased tenant had held land by the most ancient title was preferred, where the tenant had held only of *mesne* lords. Where the tenant had also held land of the king as tenant *in capite*, the king was not only entitled to wardship of the person of the heir, regardless of how many other lords there might be, but he was also entitled to wardship of all the lands that the deceased tenant had held, regardless of whom they had been held.

Sec. 12. Incidents of Tenure by Knight Service—Marriage. Another valuable and important incident of tenure that arose upon the death of a tenant leaving a minor heir or heiress was called marriage, which was the privilege of controlling the marriage of the ward. The only restraint upon the guardian in the exercise of this control was that the marriage be "without disparagement," that is, he should not marry the ward to someone of inferior rank. The right to control the marriage of males as well as of females was exercised by the guardian from the close of the twelfth century. The suitor was accustomed to offer the guardian a certain amount of money for his arranging a marriage with his ward. The heiress was not required to marry contrary to her inclination; she could purchase her freedom from the proposed marriage by the payment of an amount equal to the amount offered the guardian by the suitor. If she contracted a marriage contrary to the guardian's wishes the marriage was not void, but the guardian was entitled to compensation for the wrong that he thereby suffered. The monetary value of this incident, depending largely on the perspicacity of the guardian was highly regarded and consequently marriage became a marketable commodity. The determination of the question, as to which lord had the right of marriage where lands had been held by the deceased tenant of different lords, was settled by the determination of the question as to which lord had the right of wardship of the minor's person.

Sec. 13. Incidents of Tenure by Knight Service—Aids. The vaguely defined duty resting on the tenant to come to the lord's assistance in time of need not only in person but with money gave rise to the right of the lord to demand from the tenant, from time to time, and for certain purposes, amounts of money, known as aids. Originally, the occasions on which aids could be demanded were not fixed, but that defect was remedied by Magna Carta (1215), when the occasions on which they could be demanded were stated to be three, viz., the ransoming of the lord's person when he was held captive, the knighting of the lord's eldest son, and the marriage of the lord's eldest daughter. As to the last, the aid could only be demanded for one marriage of the daughter.

Sec. 14. Incidents of Tenure by Knight Service—Escheat —Escheat Distinguished from Forfeiture. Escheat was the final feudal incident that operated when the tenant's interest came to an end. It was classified into escheat *"propter defectum sanguinis"* and escheat *"propter delictum tenentis."* When the grantor, the lord, had given land to a man to be held by him and his heirs, if, on the death of the tenant there were no heirs, the lord was entitled to receive the land again, since the period for which he had given it had expired. On the death of the holder without heirs the land reverted to the lord through the operation of escheat *propter defectum sanguinis.* Escheat of this type depended on the existence of the tenurial relationship. As to the other type of escheat, escheat *propter delictum tenentis,* it will be remembered that when a breach of the fealty due to the lord had been committed by the tenant, it was said that the tenant had committed a "felony." Where the personal relationship was essential, as in feudal tenure, such a breach was regarded as a most heinous offense, and a tenant who had been guilty of such conduct lost his land to his lord by escheat. In the course of time, the meaning of felony was extended to cover any serious crime, and consequently, the field for the escheat of the tenant's estate was enlarged. Where escheat occurred as a consequence of a crime, however, the lord's escheat was always subject to the king's right, known as the "right of year, day and waste," which meant that the king was entitled to seize the felon's estate and use it as he pleased for that period. In later times, the lord always "compounded" for that right of the king. The right of forfeiture was not dependent on the existence of the tenurial relationship, but was rather an exercise of the prerogative right of the king to all the lands of a person convicted of high treason. When the king exercised this prerogative right, the lord was thereby deprived of his right to escheat.

B. SERJEANTY

Sec. 15. Tenure by Serjeanty. Another type of free tenure was tenure by serjeanty. Such tenure was classified into two kinds, tenure by grand serjeanty and tenure by petit serjeanty. Serjeanty meant service, and the distinguishing characteristic of the service due in this tenure was that it was pre-eminently of a personal nature. One consequence of that fact was that it was impossible to commute such services into money payment. Another was that land so held returned to the grantor on the death of the tenant, since the heir might well not be qualified to perform the personal service in return for which the land had been granted to his ancestor. By the thirteenth century, however, the heir was allowed to succeed to land held by this tenure. For the same reason lands so held were regarded as inalienable and impartible, that is, they descended to one person as heir rather than being divided among co-heirs.

Land granted by the king to members of his household in return for certain services was said to be held by grand serjeanty. Some of the grand serjeanties, which by the thirteenth century had come to be regarded as conferring dignity rather than involving menial labor were: carrying the king's banner, or his lance, or leading his army, or acting as his marshal, or as his carver, or as his butler. Likewise, there were a great number and variety of petit serjeanties connected with the humbler duties of the king's household; by conferring lands to be held by that tenure, he took care of the personal needs of himself and his household. Serjeanties might be either of a military or of a non-military nature. By military serjeanties the feudal army was supplied with light auxiliary troops, materials for war, and means of transport.

The lords naturally followed the king's example in providing for their personal needs by granting land to be held in serjeanty. It was very common for a tenant to hold land, not of the king, but of a *mesne* lord, by this type of tenure.

In the course of the fourteenth century, however, this type of tenure tended to become supplanted by the substitution of contracts with hired servants. In many cases also, tenure in serjeanty was transformed into the next type of tenure which we are to consider, tenure in free and common socage.

Sec. 16. Incidents of Tenure in Serjeanty. It was said that the same incidents that attached to tenure by knight service attached to tenure in grand serjeanty, while the incidents attaching to socage tenure attached to tenure in petit serjeanty. It may be noted that at a time when the amount of the relief payable in other tenures had become fixed, the relief payable by the heir of a tenant in serjeanty was still uncertain. In Bracton's time, about the middle of the thirteenth century, the requirement seems to have been that the relief be reasonable; later it was fixed at one year's value of the land.

C. FREE AND COMMON SOCAGE

Sec. 17. Tenure in Free and Common Socage. Socage tenure was the form of free tenure that eventually came to be of the greatest importance, displacing the other free tenures. Those who held their lands by this kind of tenure were freemen who were obliged to render service, other than military, in labor, money, produce or attendance at the lord's court. Pollock and Maitland describe this tenure as appearing, when it had attained its full compass, as the great residuary tenure, being non-military, non-serventual, and non-eleemosynary. The distinguishing characteristic of this type of tenure came to be the certainty of the services required. Gradually the services required of the tenant in socage, which had been, in the main, agricultural services, were commuted into money payments.

All of the incidents found in tenure by knight service applied to socage tenure, except wardship and marriage. The absence of these burdensome incidents was partially responsible for the eventual displacement of the other tenures by socage tenure.

Sec. 18. Incidents of Tenure in Free and Common Socage—Homage and Fealty. Although the requirement of the oath of fealty was universal, and indeed sometimes constituted the only service demanded of the tenant in socage, homage was not always required.

Sec. 19. Incidents of Tenure in Free and Common Socage—Relief. As to the payment of a relief by the heir, it is doubtful whether originally the sum paid by the heir to the lord on the death of the tenant was not rather in the nature of an *"heriot"* than a relief. An ancient custom of Teutonic origin, found in the law of Anglo-Saxon England, required a tenant holding land by any type of tenure, to return to his lord at his death an *"heriot,"* something which represented the return to the lord of the capital advanced by him. This return usually took the form of the tenant's best beast. It seems clear that the payment made by the socage tenant's heir was really a relief, from the opening years of the fourteenth century. By that time the amount had been fixed at an additional year's rent.

Sec. 20. Incidents of Tenure in Free and Common Socage—Guardianship, Aids and Escheat. We have already mentioned the fact that the burdensome incidents of wardship and marriage did not attach to socage tenure. On the death of a socage tenant, leaving a minor heir, the nearest relative who was incapable of inheriting the land, became the guardian of the minor. Unlike the guardian of a minor heir of a tenant by knight service, the guardian of the heir of a tenant in socage was required to render an accounting of the profits of the land, when his guardianship terminated, which happened when the heir reached his fifteenth year. This of course meant that the guardianship was not a marketable commodity. There was nothing resembling the incident of marriage.

Like the tenant by knight service, the socage tenant was required to render aids at the proper occasions and his tenure was also liable to escheat.

Sec. 21. Varieties of Tenure in Free and Common Socage—Tenure in Gavelkind. Two varieties of socage tenure arose due to local customary law. They raised a few new problems and acquired sufficient usage to deserve mention. The first type, localized in the county of Kent, was known as gavelkind. Originally, gavelkind had meant land which yielded rent or agricultural services but in time the term came to be restricted in meaning to the description of the customs by which, in the absence of proof to the contrary, lands in the county of Kent were presumed to be affected. Many notable customs and privileges prevailed there. Chief among them were the following. Villeinage was unknown; there was no escheat for felony; the land descended equally to all sons, rather than, as in most of England, to the eldest son alone, and a minor could alienate his property at the age of fifteen.

Sec. 22. Varieties of Tenure in Free and Common Socage—Burgage Tenure. The second of these variations from the normal socage tenure was known as burgage tenure. It was not peculiar to any one locality, but was a tenure according to the custom of the boroughs, in many of which customary rules of landholding, differing from those of the common law, had developed. Frequently there was a borough custom which permitted land to be devised, this being of importance since throughout the Middle Ages proper, the landholder was denied the power of controlling the devolution of his property after death by will. What was spoken of as "borough English" was the custom by which land descended to the youngest son, rather than to the eldest son, as it did according to the common law rules of descent.

D. FRANKALMOIGN

Sec. 23. Tenure in Frankalmoign. One other form of free tenure remains to be mentioned, tenure in frankalmoign, or free-alms. That was a form of tenure restricted to a man of religion or to a religious house. The only services required in this tenure were of a spiritual and indefinite nature, for ex-

ample, saying masses for the lord or praying for his soul.
Land might be held by that tenure, either of the king, or of a
mesne lord, but the latter was more frequently the case.
Where land was held in frankalmoign of a *mesne* lord, however, the land itself continued to be subject to the burdens of
the service in return for which it had been granted to the
mesne lord, although the tenant in frankalmoign was not
obliged to render those services, unless he had agreed expressly with his grantor that he would undertake them. It
would seem that this tenure had none of the ordinary incidents of tenure; apparently not even fealty was owed to the
lord by the tenant so holding.

Sec. 24. Contemporaneous Interests in the Land. Having noticed the types of free tenure, let us pause to apply
this system of landholding to a specific tract of land. Let us
suppose that the king made a grant of land to A to be held
by A in knight service, A's obligation being to furnish five
knights to the king when called upon to do so. A thereupon
granted four portions of his land to four individuals, who
were to serve with him as knights, in return for the land.
From the portion which he had retained, A then granted a
tract to B to be held by B in free and common socage, B's
obligation being to provide a certain number of bushels of
corn to A yearly. Another portion of the land A granted to
C, a clergyman, to be held by C in frankalmoign, C's obligation being to offer prayers for A. A would probably make a
considerable number of grants in free and common socage,
since his income largely depended on the services rendered
in return for the holdings. He might also grant a portion
of the land to X to be held in serjeanty, the service required
being of a military nature, X being obligated to provide at-
tendants for A when A went to battle. Thus various persons
had simultaneous interests in the land granted by the king
to A, and held those interests by means of various tenures,
all of the land being held by tenure by knight service, one part
in addition being held by socage tenure, another by frankalmoign, and still another by serjeanty.

Each of A's tenants in turn, might, and probably would, similarly grant portions of his land in return for services which he desired to have rendered.

Sec. 25. The Manorial Organization. After making all of the above grants, A still retained a portion of the land, called the *demesne*, on which he planned to live. This constituted a typical organization of the land, called a manor, in which A, the tenant *in capite*, had provided for most of his needs by virtue of grants he had made to tenants. To this large group of persons A was lord; they owed him fealty, but he owed them protection and consequently he established a manorial court, in which their wrongs, as between each other, could be redressed.

Sec. 26. Services—Forinsec and Intrinsec Services. Let us consider the various services imposed upon the holders of the land, and upon the land itself when various persons had interests in the same piece of land. In the case where the king granted the land to A in return for the services of five knights, A had granted a portion of that land to B to be held by B in free and common socage in return for B's rendering to A a fixed number of bushels of corn yearly. At the time when A had granted that land to B, the land was already burdened with the duty of furnishing the five knights to the king. Nothing that A and B could do would remove that burden from the land. It was, however, within their power, to settle as between themselves, which one should fulfill the obligation of furnishing the knights to the king, when the king called for their services. Suppose that it was agreed that A was to discharge the obligation, but he failed to do so. The king was not without remedy in that situation; he could seize any chattels found on the land, which would in all probability belong to B, in order to enforce the obligation that the land owed him. B then had a remedy against A by the action of *"mesne,"* since A had failed to live up to his promise to protect B from the exercise of that right on the part of the king, by discharging the obligation of furnishing the knights to the king. The action was called *mesne,* from the Latin *"medius"* be-

cause A was *mesne* between the king and B, that is, he stood
between them.

The service of furnishing the knights to the king which
was considered as binding the land itself was called *"forinsec"*
service, while the service due between A and B, by virtue of
the grant from A to B, was called *"intrinsec"* service.

Let us suppose, however, that B, instead of retaining the
entire portion of land granted him by A, granted a portion to
C, a clergyman, in return for C's prayers. When this transaction occurred, the land was bound by two *forinsec* services
from which it could not be freed by any act on the part of
B and C, namely furnishing the knights to the king, and
furnishing of corn yearly to A. As between themselves
again, B and C could decide which one was to discharge these
obligations, or *forinsec* services. The service of offering prayers for B was the new *intrinsec* service due by virtue of the
bargain between B and C. Again, in the event of failure to
perform either of the *forinsec* services, the person to whom
they were owed had the right to seize chattels found on the
land to enforce the obligation. Whether or not C could seek
redress by bringing an action of *mesne* against B would, of
course, depend on whether at the time of the conveyance of
the land, it had been agreed that B was to discharge the
forinsec services.

Sec. 27.   The Lord's Remedy of Distress. The process by
which the lord enforced the performance of either *forinsec*
or *intrinsec* services which were in arrears was called distress.
The lord would, as mentioned above, seize any chattels found
on the land. He could not sell them but could keep them until
the tenant either paid what was due or gave security to con-
test the justice of the seizure in a court of law. Certain rules
had to be observed in regard to the seizure, prescribing what
chattels could be taken, and when and where the seizure could
be made. In the latter half of the thirteenth century, every
landlord had this right of distress, or as it was also called, of
distraint, that could be exercised before he had taken any judicial action against the tenant.

So far as the land itself was concerned, it was probably felt at an early period that the non-performance of services was a cause for the forfeiture of the land. However, it was not long before there arose a very strong feeling that the lord could not dispossess the tenant without first obtaining a judgment against him. It would seem likely that where a tenant had ignored the lord's repeated demands to him to fulfill his obligation, the lord would obtain a judgment in his manorial court "abjudicating" the tenant from his holding. The royal courts, however, would not allow the lord to go that far. They would only allow him, after he had distrained the chattels found on the land, to obtain from the manorial court a judgment authorizing him to distrain the tenant of his land, but when the lord seized the land by virtue of that judgment, his rights were limited just as they were in the distraint of chattels and he was only allowed to hold the land as a means of coercing the tenant into fulfilling his obligations. Where the lord was not strong enough to maintain his own manorial court, he would not even be allowed to go that far.

E. VILLEINAGE AND MODERN TENURES

Sec. 28. Tenure in Villeinage. For the *demesne* land retained by A, agricultural laborers and personal servants were needed. A supplied these needs by granting land in villeinage, the lowest type of tenure. Up to this point, we have been concerned only with the free tenures. Tenure by villeinage was an unfree tenure. Not only the unfree man, however, but the free man as well, might hold land by that unfree tenure. The real difference between a free man so holding and an unfree man was that the free man, by surrendering his holding, could escape from the land, while the unfree man was regarded as being bound to the soil. The main distinction that resulted from tenure by villeinage as opposed to one of the free tenures, was that the king's courts, and royal justice, were available only to the man who held his land by one of the free tenures. A villein tenant, however, was not entirely without protection. The manorial court, administered by the lord, in accordance with the customs prevailing in the manor, afforded him protection which answered his needs well enough when he was denied justice by one other than the lord himself. Naturally since the lords considered that they were bound by manorial customs they took care that those customs should be recorded. "Extents" setting forth the details of each tenancy were periodically made by a sworn jury of tenants.

Sec. 29. Tenure in Villeinage—Division of the Manorial Lands. The lands of the manor were of three kinds. We have already mentioned the lord's demesne land, whereon his manor-house was situated. There were, in addition, the lands held by the lord's freehold tenants and finally, the *"villenagium,"* or the lands held by the lord's villein tenants.

The arable land of the manor was ordinarily divided into three fields, which were cultivated in a certain rotation so that each year one of the fields was allowed to lie fallow. The fields were then divided into a certain number of strips, separated by turf balks. Each landholder held a certain number of strips scattered over the various fields, the holdings probably being so allotted in order that he might have a certain amount of each kind of land. Over the field that was lying fallow, each landholder had what was spoken of as a right of *shack*, or a right to pasture his cattle there. Similarly he had rights of common over the waste lands adjoining the village.

Sec. 30. Tenure in Villeinage—Type of Services Required. In general, the service due the lord by the villein tenant was of an agricultural nature, the villein being required to devote a certain amount of labor to the cultivation of the lord's demesne lands. The work required of the villein was not uncertain in the sense that it was not definitely fixed and prescribed; it was prescribed minutely in the manorial extents, and fixed by custom. As pointed out by Pollock and Maitland,[6]

---

[6] Pollock and Maitland, History of English Law (2d ed. 1911), Vol. II, p. 353.

the uncertainty was such that the villein tenant did not know in the evening what work he might be called upon to do in the morning. The test frequently applied by the king's court in the determination of the question whether a tenant were free or unfree was whether there was any considerable uncertainty as to the kind and amount of agricultural services required. There were, however, other tests in use; for example, it was felt that any incident of the type regarded as one that would attach to a tenure unworthy of a free man, characterized the tenure as unfree. Despite the fact that this placed the cart before the horse and determined the nature of the tenure by the incidents of the relationship, it operated satisfactorily due to the existence of the manorial "extents," and the records of the manorial courts, simplifying the problem of proof when the matter was attacked in this oblique fashion. The *"merchet,"* the fine paid by the tenant on the marriage of his daughter, and sometimes on the marriage of his son, was regarded as an incident of such a nature. The villein tenant had to secure permission of his lord if his daughter were to marry outside the manor, or if his son were to be ordained. Likewise, he could not sell his horse or ox without the permission of the lord, since the stock on the tenement was not to be diminished. The liability of being *tallaged* high or low, or taxed arbitrarily by the lord, was another incident which was regarded as marking a tenure as unfree.

Sec. 31. Tenure in Villeinage—Inheritability and Alienability of Tenement. Apparently the villein tenant's rights were inheritable, and so regarded in the manorial court, at least as against every one other than the lord. On the death of the tenant, an *heriot* was due the lord. The *heriot* here retained its ancient form and generally was satisfied by the surrender of the best beast owned by the tenant. It was not regarded as a payment made by the heir for the privilege of being recognized as heir and allowed to succeed to his ancestor's interest, but rather as the payment of a debt due the lord by the deceased tenant.

The villein tenant could not alienate his land without

obtaining the lord's consent, and an attempt at alienation without that consent was cause for forfeiture of the holding.

Although the villein tenant held at the will of the lord, nevertheless it must be emphasized that the lord considered himself bound by the customs of the manor. The lord, it is true, had the power to oust his tenant, but in practice it seems that he preferred to exact a fine from an erring tenant rather than to eject him.

Sec. 32. Commutation of Services into Money Payments —Transition from Villein to Copyhold Tenure. Originally it would seem that the services required of a villein tenant were arbitrarily imposed by the lord, but as early as the thirteenth century, both the labor and money payments were definitely prescribed on the manorial "extents." In the fourteenth century the process of commuting those services into money payments began. That process, it should be noted, was one that was initiated by the lord, when it became to his advantage to substitute money payments. When the services were thus commuted, tenure in villeinage became tenure by copy of the manorial court roll, and was thereafter known as copyhold tenure.

Holdsworth finds [7] three conditions precedent for the transition from a system of natural husbandry to a system of money rents: the centralized government of England which kept the peace, the insular position of the country which protected it from foreign invasion, and the rise of the woolen industry. The Black Death, which occurred in 1348-1349 strengthened the tendency by breaking up the solidarity of the manorial organization. As he points out, all over England, following that catastrophe, tenants abandoned their lands to become hired laborers on the land, artisans, soldiers of the Crown, or paid retainers of some great lord.

Labor services in general had been commuted into money rents by the middle of the fifteenth century, thus really bring-

---

[7] Holdsworth, Historical Introduction to the Land Law (1927), pp. 42-44, incl.

ing tenure in villeinage to an end, and substituting therefor copyhold tenure. Once the agricultural services had been commuted into money payments, the king's courts no longer refused to accord protection to the tenant. There had been a reason for their refusing to accord protection to the villein tenant since for them to have done so would have meant an interference with the agricultural economy of the manor. Now that it was possible readily to ascertain the terms of the tenure by an examination of the manorial court rolls, the king's court was willing to see to it that the terms of the tenure were respected.

In the course of the sixteenth century a compromise was effected. If the land had been anciently copyhold, the lords were compelled to respect the land held by copyholders; that is, the lords had to respect the customs of the manor and the terms of the tenancy as set forth on the manorial court rolls. No land, however, was to be regarded as copyhold unless it had been so considered time out of mind. The copyhold tenant had acquired an interest protected by the royal courts, his tenure being on the terms upon which his services had been commuted into money. In the course of time, the law of copyhold was assimilated into the law of free tenure by the courts, in so far at least as the law of free tenure did not come into conflict with the customary law of the manor. When this had happened, tenure by copyhold had lost any servile taint that had once attached to it, and it survived merely as a form of landholding.

Sec. 33. Alienation of Copyhold Lands. It is notable that the copyholder, unlike the villein tenant, had a free right of alienation. The lord, however, was allowed to charge a fine upon the admittance of the new tenant and sometimes also for enrollment. The use of any other method of alienation was regarded as cause for forfeiture. Apparently at the time when copyhold was a new method of landholding, the lord actually exercised control over the selection of the person to whom a copyhold tenant could convey his interest, but by the time of

Coke, in the closing years of the sixteenth century, that discretionary power of the lord had disappeared.

Sec. 34.   Alienation of Freehold Lands by Mesne Tenant. So far we have given no attention to a very important problem, whether or not the *mesne* tenant holding land by one of the free tenures, could alienate his interest in the land without the consent of the lord. In approaching this problem, it is important to bear in mind that the oath of fealty sworn by the tenant to the lord had been an essential part in the creation of the tenure. It is necessary to consider the importance of the personal relationship thereby created between lord and tenant, when the tenant desired to transfer his entire interest to another person whom he wished to make his lord's tenant in his stead. Presumably the land had been originally granted to the tenant because the lord thought that the tenant was a person whose services would be of value to him and one who was worthy of protection in return. It is obvious that the person whom the tenant proposed to put in his place might not be one whom the lord was willing to accept as tenant. It was entirely within the realm of possibility that he might even be an enemy of the lord, in which case the oath of fealty would be a farce.

Sec. 35.   Alienation by Way of Substitution. The process of transferring a tenant's interest to another who thereby became the tenant of the lord of whom the transferor had held the land was spoken of as substitution. If, instead of transferring his entire interest, the tenant transferred only a part of his interest, remaining a tenant of the lord as to the part retained, but substituting his alienee as tenant for the part conveyed, the problem of apportioning the services due the lord arose. It must be remembered that nothing that the tenant could do, without the consent of the lord, could have the effect of freeing the *land* from the service to the lord with which it was burdened, but the lord might well object to having in the first instance to look to his grantee and one-quarter of the land for one-quarter of the services, and then to his tenant's grantee and the rest of the land for the rest of the services.

Sec. 36. Alienation by Way of Subinfeudation. The tenant, instead of desiring to transfer either a whole or a part of his interest to another, substituting that other as the lord's tenant, might wish to grant a part or all of the land to some other person who would hold the land of himself, thereby becoming not the tenant of the donor's lord, but the tenant of the donor himself. This sort of alienation was termed subinfeudation. Like substitution, subinfeudation might affect the lord disadvantageously, but in another manner. We have already spoken of the various incidents of tenure which were profitable to the lord, notably, relief, wardship, marriage and escheat. Suppose that B, who was A's tenant, proceeded to grant his entire interest or part of it, to C, who thereby became B's tenant. B might grant the land to C to be held by C for the rendering of a purely nominal service, for example, the yearly rendering of a loaf of bread, in recognition of B's lordship. The feudal incidents still remained, in favor of A; A, for instance, was entitled to relief on B's death, but since the yearly value of B's interest had been reduced to a single loaf of bread, that incident had ceased to be of value to A. So too the incidents of wardship, marriage and escheat had been rendered worthless to A, since B's interest had become purely nominal. Of course, the services by which B held the land were still due to A, but A had suffered by losing the occasional profits arising from feudal incidents that had formerly been of real value to him.

Sec. 37. Statute of Quia Emptores. There was considerable doubt until the end of the thirteenth century as to what restrictions the lord could place on the free alienation of the tenant's interest. In 1290, however, the question was settled by the passage of the Statute of Quia Emptores,[8] which provided:

---

[8] 18 Edward I (1290).

"Forasmuch as purchasers of lands and tenements of the fees of great men and other lords have many times heretofore entered into their fees, to the prejudice of the lords, to whom the freeholders of such great men have sold their lands and tenements to be holden in fee of their feoffors and not of the chief lords of the fees, whereby the same chief lords have many times lost their escheats, marriages, and wardships of lands and tenements belonging to their fees, which thing seems very hard and extreme unto these lords and other great men, and moreover in this case manifest disinheritance, our lord the king in his Parliament at Westminster after Easter the eighteenth year of his reign, this is to wit in the quinzine of Saint John Baptist, at the instance of the great men of the realm granted, provided and ordained, that from henceforth it shall be lawful to every freeman to sell at his own pleasure his lands and tenements or part of them, so that the feoffee shall hold the same lands or tenements of the chief lord of the same fee, by such services and customs as his feoffor held before.

"C.2. And if he sell any part of such lands or tenements to any, the feoffee shall immediately hold of it the chief lord, and shall be forthwith charged with the services for so much as pertaineth or ought to pertain to the said chief lord, for the same parcel, according to the quantity of the land or tenement so sold; and so in this case the same part of the service shall remain to the lord, to be taken by the hands of the feoffee, for the which he ought to be attendant and answerable to the same chief lord according to the quantity of the land or tenement sold for the parcel of the service so due."

It is clear that the statute represented a compromise. The lord conceded to the tenant the full power of alienation by way of substitution, thus incurring the disadvantages of apportionment of the services. The lord benefited by the fact that the process of alienation by subinfeudation was forbidden, and he was therefore no longer in danger of depreciation of the feudal incidents.

During the reign of Edward II, at the beginning of the fourteenth century, it was settled that the lord could not evade the statute, by charging fines upon alienation.

Sec. 38. Alienation by Tenants in Capite. Our discussion has thus far been restricted to alienation on the part of *mesne* tenants. The question also arose as to the power of alienation on the part of the tenant *in capite*. The Statute of Quia Emptores, it must be remembered, had no application to the king. He was the only one who was always lord, never tenant, and it was he who suffered from the depreciation of the feudal incidents. In 1265 a royal ordinance forbade all tenants *in capite* to alienate without royal license, but in 1327 such tenants acquired the right of free alienation on the payment of a fine.

Sec. 39. Alienation of Lordships. Another problem was whether or not the lord could transfer his lordship, without the consent of the tenant, whether the tenant could be compelled to accept a new lord. Bracton states that where a tenant has done homage to his lord, he might, for good cause, for instance, on the ground that the alienee was his personal enemy, object to having his homage transferred. So far as the service burdening the land was concerned, as opposed to the homage, that could always be transferred even against the tenant's will. There was a court process for "attorning" or turning over the tenant to the new lord. There seems to be little indication, however, that the power of the lords to alienate their lordships was ever fettered to any extent by the tenants.

Sec. 40. Alienation in Mortmain. In 1279 the power of alienating land to religious houses was restricted by the Statute of Mortmain, (mortmain meaning a dead hand), which prevented the indiscriminate grant of lands to religious bodies. The result of the statute was to decrease tenure in frankalmoign. This tenure was undesirable from the point of view of the feudal incidents. When land was so held, the lord had, in the person of the religious corporation, a tenant who was never under age, never married, never committed treason and never died. The Statute of Quia Emptores of 1290 contained this section:

> "C.3. And it is to be understood that by the said sales and purchases of lands or tenements, or any parcel of them, such lands or tenements shall in no wise come into mortmain, either in part or in whole, neither by policy nor craft, contrary to the form of the statute thereupon of late."

After the passage of that statute, no new grants of land to be held in frankalmoign or to be held in any other tenure by a religious body could be made except by the king to whom the statute was not applicable.

Sec. 41. Statute of Tenures. A great change was effected in the law relating to tenures and tenurial incidents by the Statute of Tenures,[9] enacted in 1660, during the reign of Charles II. That statute read:

> "Whereas it hath been found by former experience that the Court of Wards and Liveries and tenure by knight-service either of the king or others, or by knight-service *in capite,* or socage *in capite,* of the king, and the consequents upon the same, have been much more burthensome, grievous and prejudicial to the kingdom than they have been beneficial to the king; and whereas since the intermission of the said court, which hath been from the four and twentieth day of February, which was in the year of our Lord one thousand six hundred forty and five, many persons have by will and otherwise made disposal their lands held by knight-service, whereupon divers questions might possibly arise unless some seasonable remedy be taken to prevent the same; be it therefore enacted by the King our Sovereign Lord, with the assent of the Lords and Commons in Parliament assembled, and by the author-

---

[9] 12 Carolus II, c. 24, Statute Abolishing the Court of Wards and Liveries (1660).

ity of the same, and it is hereby enacted, That the
Court of Wards and Liveries, and all wardships, liveries, primer seisins and *ousterlemains,* values and forfeitures of marriages, by reason of any tenure of
the King's Majesty, or of any other by knight-service,
and all mean rates, and all other gifts, grants, and
charges, incident or arising for or by reason of wardships, liveries, primer seisins, or *ousterlemains* be
taken away and discharged, and are hereby enacted
to be taken away and discharged, from the said twenty-
fourth day of February one thousand six hundred
forty-five; any law, statute, custom, or usage to the
contrary hereof in any wise notwithstanding: And that
all fines for alienation, seizures, and pardons for alienations, tenure by homage, and all charges incident or
arising for or by reason of wardship, livery, primer
seisin, or *ousterlemain,* or tenure by knight-service,
escuage and also *aide pur file marrier, et pur faire fitz
chivalier,* and all other charges incident thereunto, be
likewise taken away and discharged from the said
twenty-fourth day of February one thousand six hundred forty and five: any law, statute, custom, or usage
to the contrary hereof in any wise notwithstanding:
And that all tenures by knight-service of the king, or
of any other person, and by knight-service *in capite,*
and by socage *in capite* of the king, and the fruits and
consequents thereof, happened or which shall or may
hereafter happen or arise thereupon or thereby, be
taken away and discharged; any law, statute, custom
or usage to the contrary hereof in any wise notwithstanding: And all tenures of any honours, manors,
land, tenements, or hereditaments, or any estate of any
inheritance at the common law, held either of the
king or of any other person or persons, bodies politick
or corporate, are hereby enacted to be turned into free
and common socage, to all intents and purposes, from
the said twenty-fourth day of February one thousand
six hundred forty-five, and shall be so construed, adjudged and deemed to be from the said twenty-fourth
day of February one thousand six hundred forty-five,

and for ever thereafter, turned into free and common socage; any law, statute, custom or usage to the contrary hereof in any wise notwithstanding.

"2. And that the same shall forever hereafter stand and be discharged of all tenure by homage, escuage, voyages royal, and charges for the same, wardships incident to tenure by knight-service, and values and forfeitures of marriage, and all other charges incident to tenure by knight-service, and of and from *aide pur file marrier*, and *aide pur faire fitz chivalier*: any law, statute, usage, or custom to the contrary in any wise notwithstanding. And that all conveyances and devises of any manors, lands, tenements, and hereditaments, made since the said twenty-fourth day of February, shall be expounded to be of such effect as if the same manors, lands, tenements, and hereditaments had been then held and continued to be holden in free and common socage only; any law, statute, custom, or usage to the contrary hereof in any wise notwithstanding.

"3. And be it further ordained and enacted by the authority of this present Parliament, That one Act made in the reign of King Henry the Eighth, entitled An Act for the Establishment of the Court of the King's Wards; and also one Act of Parliament made in the thirty-third year of the reign of the said King Henry the Eighth, concerning the officers of the Courts of Wards and Liveries, and every clause, article, and matter in the said acts contained, shall from henceforth be repealed and utterly void.

"4. And be it further enacted by the authority aforesaid, That all tenures hereafter to be created by the King's Majesty, his heirs or successors, upon any gifts or grants of any manors, lands, tenements or hereditaments, of any estate of inheritance at the common law, shall be in free and common socage, and shall be adjudged to be in free and common socage only, and not by knight-service, or *in capite* and shall be discharged of all wardship, value and forfeiture of marriage, livery, primer seisin, *ousterlemain, aide pur faire fitz chivalier* and *pur file marrier;* any law, statute, or reservation to the contrary thereof in any wise notwithstanding.

"5. Provided, nevertheless, and be it enacted, "That this Act, or anything therein contained, shall not take away, nor be construed to take away, any rents certain, heriots, or suits of court, belonging or incident to any former tenure now taken away or altered by virtue of this Act, or other services incident or belonging to tenure in common socage due or to grow due to the King's Majesty, or mean lords, or other private person, or the fealty and distresses incident thereunto; and that such relief shall be paid in respect of such rents as is paid in case of a death of a tenant in common socage.

"6. Provided always, and be it enacted, that anything herein contained shall not take away, nor be construed to take away, any fines for alienation due by particular customs of particular manors and places, other than fines for alienation of lands or tenements holden immediately of the king *in capite.*

"7. Provided also, and be it further enacted, That this Act or anything herein contained, shall not take away, or be construed to take away, tenures in frankalmoign, or to subject them to any greater or other services than they now are; nor to alter or change any tenure by copy of court-roll, or any services incident thereunto; nor to take away the honorary services of grand serjeanty other than of wardship, marriage, and value of forfeiture of marriage, escuage, voyages royal, and other charges incident to tenure by knightservice; and other than *aide pur faire fitz chivalier,* and *aide pur file marrier.*"

By the Act of 1660, then, tenure by knight service was converted into socage tenure, and scutage and homage were abolished, along with the incidents of wardship, marriage, primer seisin, aids, and fines for alienation. The other free tenures were affected by the statute only in so far as they had been subject to the feudal incidents which were abolished. The Act was stated not to apply at all to copyhold tenure.

Thus the feudal incidents which remained were of innocuous types, those incident to copyhold and socage tenures. There was still the possibility of escheat upon conviction of felony. The personal services had practically all been commuted into the payment of money, generally small sums, known as quit rents. The lord still retained his right to relief on intestate succession, and also his power of distraint.

Sec. 42. Tenure in the United States Prior to the Revolution.[10] Turning to the United States, it is unquestionable that the grants of lands in colonial America were made to be held in free and common socage, some nominal service, for instance, the annual render of two beaver skins generally being reserved in the patents. The only significant elements of the colonial socage tenure were fealty, escheat, quit rents and the lord's power of distress, and only the latter two, quit rents and the power of distress to enforce their collection, became of real importance in the colonies.

Sec. 43. Tenure in the New England Colonies. It is easy to understand why the payment of quit rents and the lord's power of distraint were highly obnoxious to the New England settlers, who had left England because they were unwilling to submit to restraints imposed upon them by others. There is therefore nothing surprising in finding that the New Englanders determinedly resisted any effort to collect such rents, and that they had, long before the Revolution, succeeded in establishing free tenure over the whole of New England.

Sec. 44. Tenure in New York and the Southern Colonies. In New York, and the colonies to the south, although resentment was aroused by the collection of quit rents and although there was some resistance thereto, the right of the lords to collect such rents and to distrain when they were not paid,

---

[10] The material dealing with tenure in the United States is largely taken from the excellent article by Vance, The Quest for Tenure in the United States, (1923) 33 Yale L.J. pp. 248-271.

continued to be recognized almost to the time of the Revolution, as did the lords' right to escheats and fines upon alienation. In those colonies, the main difficulty seems to have arisen over the fact that there was a very strong feeling on the part of the colonists that the revenue from rents so collected should not be used for any other than governmental purposes.

Sec. 45. **Tenure in the United States Following the Revolution.** After the Revolution, there was a universal desire on the part of the states to do away entirely with the claims of the lords. New England had already attained the desirable result. In the majority of the other states it was now accomplished by the passage of statutes abolishing feudal tenures or declaring all lands to be alodial. Three states, Delaware, North Carolina and Georgia, never troubled to enact such statutes, but nevertheless reached the same result, in the absence of legislation.

Sec. 46. **Tenure in Pennsylvania and South Carolina.** In two states alone, Pennsylvania and South Carolina, does feudal tenure still appear to exist. Pennsylvania in 1779, passed a "Divesting Act," confiscating the rights and abolishing the political powers of the proprietaries, but it seems settled that that act did not destroy feudal tenure.[11] Moreover, the Statute of Quia Emptores was never in force in Pennsylvania, with the result that rent reserved, even on a grant in fee, is rent service, apportionable and enforceable by distress. Pennsylvania has never, either by statute or constitutional provision, abolished feudal tenures or declared lands to be alodial.

Sec. 47. **Incidents of Tenure in the United States.** In the United States, where the state is the only overlord, the incidents of tenure have either ceased to exist or have ceased

---

[11] There has been considerable disagreement in Pennsylvania on this point. Wallace v. Harmstad, 44 Pa. 492 (1863) (all tenure is alodial). The better opinion is contrary to this case and in accord with the position taken in the text. See Sharswood, Law Lectures (1870), VII, VIII; Mitchell, The Law of Real Estate, etc., in Pennsylvania (1890), 77-78.

to be of any significance. The oath of allegiance which is due from the holder of land, only as it is due from any other citizen, has supplanted the oath of fealty. Homage has vanished. Escheat is still with us under the same name, though necessarily under a different theory, but forfeiture does not exist. Wardships and marriages are alike unknown to our system. The control which our state governments take over minors is very similar from the standpoint of the power concept, but there is within it no comparable concept of privilege that the guardian make profit from the affairs of the minor.

Fines for alienation of land find an analogy in stamp taxes and recording and registration fees exacted at the time of a conveyance. Forinsec services and aids have a counterpart in the present day taxes on land. Primer seisin and reliefs are represented today by modern inheritance taxes.

Distress as a common law power incident to tenure of land in fee continues today only in Pennsylvania, and exists in other states only in statutory form, to compel the payment of rent by the tenant in a landlord and tenant relationship.

While the state has the power of eminent domain, that power has always been recognized, not as an incident of tenure, but as one of the prerogatives of sovereignty.

BIBLIOGRAPHY

Blackstone, Sir William, Commentaries on the Laws of England, Book II, c. IV * 44-53, c. V * 61-77, c. VI * 78-101.

Digby, Kenelm Edward, An Introduction to the History of the Law of Real Property (5th ed. 1897), pp. 1-61, 76-94, 100-105, 120-127, 131-133, 136-144, 152-161, 212-222, 234-239, 288-297, 393-400.

Holdsworth, W. S., An Historical Introduction to the Land Law (1927), pp. 16-19, 21-48, 102-110, 118-119, 131-136.

Holdsworth, W. S., A History of the English Law (4th ed. 1931), Vol. I, pp. 179-185; Vol. II, pp. 56-63, 370-371, 379-381; Vol. III, pp. 29-87, 171-185, 198-213, 217-234, 246-248, 256-275; Vol. VII, pp. 296-312, 356-362.

Pollock and Maitland, The History of English Law Before the Time of Edward I (2d ed. 1911), Vol. I, pp. 207-389; Vol. II, pp. 192-193, 573-576.

Vance, The Quest for Tenure in the United States, (1923) 33 Yale L.J. pp. 248-271.

CHAPTER II

ESTATES IN LAND

Sec. 48. The Development of the Estate Concept. The development of the word "estate" into its present meaning in Anglo-American law is in itself an interesting commentary on the development of our real property law. The word itself stemmed from the Latin word *"status."* As has been pointed out in the preceding chapter dealing with feudal tenure, the landholding system was originally simply a point of reference for an organization which was purely political in character. A man's position in this organization was his status, connoting various personal relationships to those above and below him, and by virtue of this status he held a certain amount of land under one of the forms of tenure, so limited as to endure for a longer or shorter period. The duration and the form of tenure were both results of his status—his personal position. In Bracton's time, about the thirteenth century, the word status was still used in this sense. Subsequently, as the political organization based on the land proved inefficient and was superseded by a much more centralized form of government, the law of real property had to develop out of the relics of this broken political organization. Status obviously had to lose its original meaning since the organization no longer functioned. It was at this period that the peculiar inversion of the usage of the term status to signify those relationships with reference to land which had originally been the by-products of the status itself arose. Our present day concept of an estate in land is a concept in which an individual has, with reference to the land, and to innumerable other individuals, certain rights, privileges, powers and immunities. The peculiar combination of those rights, privileges, powers and immunities measures the extent of the estate and permits us to classify estates. By using this concept, and envisaging an interest in the land which is separate from the land itself, it is possible for many persons simultaneously to have estates in the same tract of land. The concept then is projected, as pointed out by Pollock and Maitland,[1] upon a plane of time so that with reference to the one piece of land some estates may be spoken of as possessory estates, or estates of present enjoyment, others as expectant estates, or estates of future enjoyment.

A. ESTATES OF PRESENT ENJOYMENT

I. Freehold Estates

Sec. 49. Distinction between Freehold and Non-freehold Estates. Interests are classified as either freehold or non-freehold interests. The freehold estates were the favored interests of the law, the holders of which were accorded full protection in the king's court by the real actions. The basis of the distinction between such interests and the non-freehold interests is shrouded in the murky gloom of mediaeval legal history. Investigation of the various theories explaining this distinction would, for our purposes, be rather fruitless. It is sufficient that we recognize the characteristic variation between the two types. The duration of freehold estates is always an uncertain period—so long as a man's heirs endure, so long as the heirs of his body endure, or so long as a man lives. Such freehold estates are estates in fee simple, estates in fee tail and life estates. The non-freehold estates which are con-

---

[1] Pollock and Maitland, The History of English Law Before the Time of Edward I (2d ed. 1911), 10.

sidered lower in the real property scale always have a definite period of termination. These interests are: terms for years, tenancy at will, periodic tenancy and tenancy at sufferance.

a. Fee Simple

Sec. 50. Estate in Fee Simple Absolute—Nature and Incidents. Much concerning the nature of landholdings shortly after the Norman Conquest is extremely doubtful. It is generally assumed, however, that originally all of the landholding was limited in its duration to the life of the first taker. The reasons for this are obvious. Since the landholding depended on the status of the individual, and status was a personal relationship, there would be no reason to suppose that by the mere accident of birth a worthy successor to the present holder of any particular status would be provided. A man held land because he was a good knight or a good cook; it was quite within the realm of possibility that the knight's son might be a coward and the cook's son a person temperamentally unsuited to the preparation of gastronomic delights.

Two factors combined to lessen the importance of the personal relationship and as a result change the method of landholding. The overlords of the feudal period seem frequently to have been in necessitous circumstances, due to the expensive wars of the time. Their armies, also, were not dependable, due to the difficulty of obtaining the personal services when and where they were needed. To remedy these conditions, personal services were gradually commuted into money payments. This removed the principal objection to the inheritance of landholdings. In addition, the lords saw the inheritance as a new source of revenue, through the exaction of a money payment called the relief on the heir's being permitted to take up the inheritance. Gradually, landholdings became inheritable due to these reasons.

Sec. 51. Fee Simple Absolute at Common Law—Creation. As a result of the change in the nature of landholding, the custom gradually arose of indicating in the gift to the first taker that the land should be inheritable, by stating that the land was given "to A and his heirs." Since the land was being given, and necessarily the donor was bound only by what he said he was giving, the inclusion of this term became essential to an inheritable interest in the land. Extreme formalism is a characteristic of all early forms of law. As a result, no other phrase could take the place of the magic words "and his heirs" in a conveyance *inter vivos*. After land became devisable by will (1540) a fee simple could be created by will without using these words.

Sec. 52.   **Fee Simple Absolute—Nature of the Heir's Interest.** The next question to arise would naturally be—does the addition of these words confer any interest, in itself, upon the heirs, or the presumptive heirs of the first taker? It seems clear that in the eleventh and twelfth centuries the presumptive heirs were regarded as taking an interest by virtue of being mentioned in the gift. This is evidenced by the fact that in Glanvil's time at the close of the twelfth century, the consent of the presumptive heirs was essential to the validity of a conveyance by the first taker. The courts, however, throughout English history, have been the liberal group contending against the conservative landholding families in breaking down restraints on the alienation of land. The entire history of real property could be written in terms of the conflict between these two tendencies and the two groups upholding them. It is notable throughout our history that every restraint upon the alienation of a type of interest originated by the class of great landowners has been gradually eaten away by a course of fine-spun decisions until land has once more become the subject of free commerce in the market place. By the early part of the thirteenth century, the courts had decided that the words "and his heirs" created no interest in the heirs and thus this particular restraint upon alienation was demolished.

The legal expression "and his heirs" still had a definite value in the conveyance, but that value was not in creating an interest in the presumptive heirs of the first taker, but in creating a durability in the estate of the first taker—delimiting the first taker's interest as one that would continue beyond his lifetime and descend to his heirs. The heirs, however, clearly were taking by "descent" from the first taker rather than by "purchase" from the original donor. "Purchase" in legal contemplation should not be confused with purchase in its non-legal sense. A "purchaser" in law is anyone who takes directly from the grantor by virtue of a gift to him in the conveyance.

This is the estate in fee simple as it is known in English law. It is an interest in the land of potentially infinite duration. On the death of the first taker it will pass successively to all those persons who by the rules of descent are his heirs-at-law. These heirs-at-law will include both his direct descendants and those persons who are related to him only collaterally.

Sec. 53. Fee Simple Absolute—Alienability. The first taker can also freely alienate this interest without obtaining anyone's consent. Such alienation, however, raises a very nice problem. Since the gift was "to A and his heirs," and the duration of the estate was so long as A should have heirs, if A conveys to B and at some subsequent time, all of A's heirs die out, does B's estate thereupon terminate? By the time of Bracton, in the middle of the thirteenth century, it was settled that an estate in fee simple would endure until the person entitled to it for the time being, whether he were the original grantee or an alienee, died leaving no heir.

Sec. 54. Fee Simple Absolute—Devolution on Death. This complete power of alienation on the part of the holder in fee simple was limited, however, to an *inter vivos* transaction. Until the passage of the Statute of Wills in 1540, except in a few localities by virtue of a peculiar custom, it was impossible to make a will which would pass title to real property. On the death of the holder in fee simple, the interest was bound to descend to his heirs, and since alienations in this period were extremely infrequent the heir's chance of getting the interest was an excellent one. After the passage of the Statute of Wills, the holder of the interest could control the disposition of the land not only by an *inter vivos* transaction, but also after death by means of his will.

Sec. 55. Fee Simple Absolute—Position of the Holder of the Interest. The foregoing were the very ample powers which the holder of a fee simple had over the interest. In addition, he had other powers, and a great many rights, privileges and immunities. He possessed the totality of these relations with reference to the land permissible under the law. He had the privilege of exclusive enjoyment and might use the land in any way and for any purpose he saw fit. He was immune from all control in the enjoyment of his interest in his real property save that control exercised by the State for the protection of society in general. Should he die without having disposed of his interest by will, and leaving no heirs, direct or collateral, the State (occupying the position of the lord) succeeded to his interest by escheat. The State then held the interest in fee simple just as had the deceased with exactly the same rights, privileges, powers and immunities.

Sec. 56. Fee Simple Absolute in the United States—Creation. The rule of the common law that in order to create an estate in fee simple by conveyance *inter vivos,* the conveyance must be made to the grantee "and his heirs" has been eliminated by statute in nearly all of the states.[2] The substance of these statutes generally is that any conveyance by a person owning an estate in fee simple transfers an estate in fee simple unless an intent is expressed to transfer an estate of a different type. Statutes of this type relating both to deeds and wills are in force in thirty-five states and the District of Columbia. The thirty-five states are: Alabama, Arizona, California, Colorado, Georgia, Idaho, Illinois, Indiana, Kansas, Kentucky, Maryland, Massachusetts, Michigan, Minnesota, Mississippi, Missouri, Montana, Nebraska, Nevada, New Jersey, New York, North Carolina, North Dakota, Ohio, Oklahoma, Oregon, Rhode Island, Tennessee, Texas, Utah, Virginia, Washington, West Virginia, Wisconsin, and Wyoming. In Arkansas, Florida, Pennsylvania, and Iowa the statute applies

---

[2] American Law Institute, Restatement of Property, Tentative Draft No. 1, secs. 48 and 49, pp. 98-102. Explanatory Notes on Tentative Draft No. 1, pp. 22-29. Proposed Final Draft, secs. 48 and 49, pp. 115-121.

to conveyances by deed only, while in Delaware, Maine, New Hampshire, South Carolina, South Dakota, and Vermont the statute is applicable only to wills. In addition, South Dakota has a statute providing that the expressed intent of the grantor controls, that technical words of inheritance are not necessary. The statute applies only to deeds. Iowa also has an additional similar statute, which applies only to wills.

Sec. 57. Methods of Conveyance of Estates in Fee Simple Absolute at Common Law—Feoffment with Livery of Seisin. The commonest type of conveyance used at common law to transfer an estate in fee simple had its roots in the formalism and simplicity of the ideas of the period. To the mind of the mediaeval lawyer, a transfer without some physical evidence of transfer was inconceivable. The result was the feoffment with livery of seisin. The feoffment consisted of two parts. It was essential that there be words of donation expressing the nature and extent of the interest to be taken by the feoffee, and that there be "livery of seisin," the ceremony fixed upon by the law for passing seisin, or possession, from the feoffor to the feoffee. Livery of seisin was performed by taking the grantee upon the land and there making a symbolical delivery of the land itself by manual delivery of a clod of earth or a twig. However, it was considered sufficient if the two parties were actually present on the land and the feoffor gave the feoffee possession by word or by deed. It was even effectual for the feoffor to bring the feoffee within sight of the land and there give him authority to enter, provided that entry was actually made subsequently by the feoffee during the life of the feoffor. The notoriety of the transaction was of the greatest importance. In the Teutonic Law, which made use of the same method of conveyance, the older law books are illustrated, and from the *Sachsenspiegel,* the oldest Teutonic law book, we know that in making the livery of seisin, it was customary to gather up half a dozen small boys from the neighborhood and compel them to stand by and watch the actual delivery. At the termination of the ceremony, the feoffor would give each boy a vigorous clout across the side of the head, so that the occasion would be impressed upon his memory. The youth of the witnesses assured the longevity of the recollection. It was of the utmost importance for all the neighbors to know that A was tenant to B from the fact that open livery of seisin had been made. The notoriety of the transaction was necessary to B in order to enable him to protect and assert his rights as lord. Feoffment with livery of seisin was the only type of conveyance used for several centuries. The long continuance of this mode of conveyance is ascribed by Holdsworth [3] partly to the fact that it helped to promote publicity and thus to prevent frauds, and partly to the fact that the procedure in the real actions, or actions relating to land, necessitated the presence of a tenant who was seised. Gradually writing to evidence the intent with which livery of seisin had been made became common, but livery of seisin alone was sufficient without a writing until the passage of the Statute of Frauds in 1677.

Sec. 58. Methods of Conveyance of Estates in Fee Simple Absolute at Common Law—the Exchange. To conveyances by way of feoffment with livery of seisin may be added conveyances by way of exchange. An exchange was a mutual grant of equal interests in lands, the one being made in consideration of the other. The equality required was an equality of quantum and interest, not of value. A might in that way exchange his estate in fee simple in Blackacre with B's estate in fee simple in Whiteacre, and in any event the estates had to be of the same type as life estate for life estate, lease for years for lease for years. Although this could be done by simple deed, unaccompanied by livery of seisin, the transaction was not perfected until both of the parties had actually entered upon the lands.

Sec. 59. Methods of Conveyance of Estates in Fee Simple Absolute at Common Law—the Release. A common law conveyance called the release was originally used for the purpose of conveying an interest of future enjoyment to the holder

---

[3] Holdsworth, An Historical Introduction to the Land Law (1927), 113.

of an interest of present enjoyment in the same land. Of course this interest of future enjoyment could itself be an estate in fee simple. The release, which required no livery of seisin, and which was normally in writing, was effective in conveying an estate in fee simple, although that estate was not presently seised. Later this type of conveyance came to be used to convey any interest in fee simple when the title was not clear, since in that situation it was quite possible either that the grantor would be out of possession or in danger of losing his possession.

Sec. 60. Methods of Conveyance of Estates in Fee Simple Absolute at Common Law—Lease and Release. Another method of conveyancing developed at common law and stemming directly from the availability of a release to convey an estate in fee simple not in possession to one having a possessory interest was the lease and release. In this type of conveyance the grantor would first execute a conveyance of a leasehold to the alienee, who would then have to take possession of the land in order to validate the lease. The grantor would thereupon convey his non-possessory interest in fee simple to the lessee by means of a release. The lessee would then have both interests amounting to a complete fee simple.

Sec. 61. Disadvantage of Common Law Methods of Conveyancing. In all these methods of conveying a fee simple at common law is found the same disadvantage. Either the grantor or the grantee, or both, depending upon the type of conveyance employed, had actually to enter upon the land or at least go in sight of it to complete the effectiveness of the conveyance. In many cases this was obviously inconvenient.

Sec. 62. Development of Equitable Estates. Simultaneously with the development of these common law methods of conveying an estate in land two methods developed of creating or conveying equitable estates, i.e., estates not recognized by the courts of law but only by another system of courts, the courts of equity. Briefly the development of these equitable estates and of the methods of conveying them was as follows:

The Church was a very strong factor in England during

the mediaeval period. It maintained its own courts which took unto themselves the control of all human conduct, any of the consequences of which could be termed spiritual. The custom gradually arose of conveying land by one of the common law methods mentioned above to a person whom the grantor trusted, at the same time directing him to hold the title for the benefit of the grantor or of some other person named at the time of the conveyance. The alienee, known as the feoffee to uses, was, so far as the law courts were concerned, the holder of the fee simple title. The directions to hold the land for the benefit of someone else were entirely ignored by these courts, but since the feoffee to uses was bound on his honor to permit the grantor or the person named to enjoy the land, and any breach of his obligation would be a violation of a duty of conscience and thus a spiritual matter, the ecclesiastical courts would compel the feoffee to uses to observe the conditions of the conveyance. They could not enforce this obligation by any temporal punishment but they had at their command the interdict and the excommunication which condemned the transgressor to pain for eternity so that their execution, although spiritual, was extremely effective. The result of such a conveyance was the creation of an interest which could be disposed of freely and without the necessity of going upon the land. The alienee of such an interest was protected. It was not an interest in the land itself since the law courts refused to recognize it, but for all practical purposes the holder of the "use" was the landowner.

About the fourteenth century a new officer appeared and became very prominent in the administration of justice. Prior to that time when a person had felt aggrieved and had been unable to obtain redress through the law courts he had petitioned the king for relief. As the king's realm expanded, this type of business so increased in volume that the king found it necessary to delegate a member of his personal staff to examine the petitions and extend relief in his name. The officer he selected was his chaplain who already had the duty of bestowing alms on the needy and was called the king's almoner. The chaplain now acquired a new title. From this time on, he was called the Chancellor. Being a clergyman, it was only natural that he should enforce the rights which the ecclesiastical courts enforced, and he had at his command not merely spiritual sanctions but very temporal dungeons and torture. Thus as the power of religious belief began to lose some of its force, a new method appeared of enforcing uses. The Chancellor and his assistants came to be called the court of Chancery or the court of Equity, and consequently the estates which they protected were called equitable estates.

Sec. 63. Methods of Conveying Equitable Estates—Bargain and Sale. The court of Chancery always purported to conduct itself upon a higher moral plane than the courts of law, the Chancellor being referred to as the "keeper of the king's conscience." As a consequence of this, one of the basic tenets of the court of Chancery was that Equity considered done that which should be done. When A held land to the use of B and for a valuable consideration, B contracted to convey that interest to C, or when the holder of a fee simple estate recognized by the courts of law contracted to convey to C, and C paid valuable consideration, the court of Equity applied this principle and recognized C as the holder of the use or equitable estate. This transaction was called a bargain and sale. Note however that this result followed only where there had been a valuable consideration, otherwise the court felt no compulsion to act. Gradually these transactions became so common that if a common law conveyance were brought before the equity court in which no express mention was made of a use party and no consideration was stated as having been paid, the court of Chancery would hold that a feoffor in the common law conveyance had a use which they called a resulting use. The court could not conceive of a common law conveyance without a use.

Sec. 64. Methods of Conveying Equitable Estates—Covenant to Stand Seised. Another type of conveyance of the equitable estate which the court of Chancery recognized was the covenant to stand seised. The same basic principle of

Equity, viz., that Equity considered done what should be done, enabled the court to reach this result. If A held property to the use of B, a close relative, or if X held an estate recognized by the courts of law, and purported to convey the estate to a close relative, the court would apply the maxim and recognize that close relative as the holder of the equitable estate. Here there was no valuable consideration to impel the count of conscience to action. Instead the court recognized what is called "good" consideration which was a blood or marriage relationship.

Sec. 65. Statute of Uses. In the reign of Henry VIII, for various reasons, the most important of which was the desire to restore the royal revenues, the Statute of Uses was enacted. It read as follows:[4]

"Where by the common laws of this realm, lands, tenements, and hereditaments be not devisable by testament, (2) nor ought to be transferred from one to another, but by solemn livery and seisin, matter of record writing sufficient made *bona fide,* without covin or fraud; (3) yet nevertheless divers and sundry imaginations, subtle inventions and practices have been used, whereby the hereditaments of this realm have been conveyed from one to another by fraudulent feoffments, fines, recoveries and other assurances craftily made to secret uses, intents and trusts; (4) and also by wills and testaments, sometime made by nude parols and words, sometime by signs and tokens, and sometime by writing, and for the most part made by such persons as be visited with sickness, in their extreme agonies and pains, or at such time as they have scantly had any good memory or remembrance; (5) at which times they being provoked by greedy and covetous persons lying in wait about them, do many times dispose indiscreetly and unadvisedly their lands and inheritances; (6) by reason whereof, and by occasion of which fraudulent feoffments, fines, recoveries and other like assurances to uses, confidences and trusts, divers and many heirs

---

[4] 27 Henry VIII, c. 10. An Act Concerning Uses and Wills (1536).

have been unjustly at sundry times disinherited, the
lords have lost their wards, marriages, reliefs, harriots,
escheats, aids *pur fair fils chivalier & pur file marier,*
(7) and scantly any person can be certainly assured of
any lands by them purchased, nor know surely against
whom they shall use their actions or executions for
their rights, titles and duties; (8) also men married
have lost their tenancies by the curtesy, (9) women
their dowers, (10) manifest perjuries by trial of such
secret wills and uses have been committed; (11) the
King's Highness hath lost the profits and advantages
of the lands of persons attainted, (12) and of the lands
craftily put in feoffments to the uses of aliens born,
(13) and also the profits of waste for a year and a day
of lands of felons attainted, (14) and the lords their
escheats thereof; (15) and many other inconveniences
have happened and daily do increase among the King's
subjects, to their great trouble and inquietness, and to
the utter subversion of the ancient common laws of
this realm; (16) for the extirping and extinguishment
of all such subtle practiced feoffments, fines, recoveries,
abuses and errors heretofore used and accustomed in
this realm, to the subversion of the good and ancient
laws of the same, and to the intent that the King's
Highness, or any other his subjects of this realm, shall
not in any wise hereafter by any means or inventions be
deceived, damaged or hurt, by reason of such trusts,
uses or confidences: (17) it may please the King's most
royal majesty, That it may be enacted by his Highness,
by the assent of the Lords Spiritual and Temporal, and
the Commons, in this present Parliament assembled,
and by the authority of the same, in manner and form
following; that is to say, That where any person or
persons stand or be seised, or at any time hereafter
shall happen to be seised, of and in any honours, castles,
manors, lands, tenements, rents, services, reversions,
remainders or other hereditaments, to the use, confidence or trust of any other person or persons, or of
any body politick, by reason of any bargain, sale, feoffment, fine, recovery, covenant, contract, agreement, will
or otherwise, by any manner means whatsoever it be;

that in every such case, all and every such person and persons, and bodies politick, that have or hereafter shall have any such use, confidence or trust, in fee simple, fee tail, for term of life or for years, or otherwise, or any use, confidence or trust, in remainder or reverter, shall from henceforth stand and be seised, deemed and adjudged in lawful seisin, estate and possession of and in the same honours, castles, manors, lands, tenements, rents, services, reversions, remainders and hereditaments, with their appurtenances, to all intents, constructions and purposes in the law, of and in such like estates as they had or shall have in use, trust or confidence of or in the same; (19) and that the estate, title, right and possession that was in such person or persons that were, or hereafter shall be seised of any lands, tenements or hereditaments, to the use, confidence or trust of any such person or persons, or of any body politick, be from henceforth clearly deemed and adjudged to be in him or them that have, or hereafter shall have, such use, confidence or trust, after such quality, manner, form and condition as they had before, in or to the use, confidence or trust that was in them . . ."

Sec. 66. Effect of the Statute of Uses on Conveyancing. The operation of the statute was extremely simple. If a conveyance was made by virtue of which before the statute one person would have held a freehold estate to the use of another, the statute took the legal estate from the feoffee to uses and conferred it on the person in whose favor the use was held. This was known as "executing the use."

In enacting the statute, the legislators probably did not realize that in addition to the result at which they were aiming, they were going to revolutionize the art of conveyancing. Let us see what the statute does. A, the holder of an estate in fee simple, by a bargain and sale on a valuable consideration creates a use in B. The statute immediately executes the use and places legal title in B. This consequence flows automatically from the operation of the statute, although neither A nor B have gone upon the land or been anywhere near the land.

The consequence would have been the same of course, had A used a covenant to stand seised in favor of some close relative instead of the bargain and sale with a valuable consideration in favor of a stranger. As a consequence an estate could now be conveyed without the inconvenience of a trip to the land itself.

Sec. 67. Statute of Enrollments. The conveyancing consequence of the Statute of Uses was realized shortly after its passage and since one of the apparent motivating factors in favor of the passage of the statute had been the desire to make impossible the secret passage of title which could so readily be made a vehicle of fraud, another statute, called the Statute of Enrollments, was enacted within six months. The statute read as follows:[5]

"Be it enacted by the authority of this present Parliament, That from the last day of July, which shall be in the year of our Lord God 1536, no manors, lands, tenements or other hereditaments, shall pass, alter or change from one to another whereby any estate of inheritance or freehold shall be made or take effect in any person or persons, or any use thereof to be made, by reason only of bargain and sale thereof, except the same bargain and sale be made by writing indented sealed, and enrolled in one of the King's courts of record at Westminster, (2) or else within the same county or counties where the same manors, lands or tenements, so bargained and sold, lie or be, before the *Custos Rotulorum* and two justices of the peace, and the clerk of the peace of the same county or counties, or two of them at the least, whereof the clerk of the peace to be one; (3) and the same enrolment to be had and made within six months next after the date of the same writings indented; (4) the same *Custos Rotulorum,* or justices of the peace and clerk taking for the enrolment of every such writing indented before them, where the land comprised in the same writing exceeds not the yearly value of forty shillings, ii s. that is to say xij. d.

---

5 27 Henry VIII, c. 16 (1536).

to the justices and xij. d. to the clerk; (5) and for the enrolment of every such writing indented before them, wherein the land comprised exceeds the sum of xl. s. in the yearly value, v.s. that is to say, ii. s. vi. d. to the said justices, and ii. s. vi. d. to the said clerk for the enrolling of the same; (6) and that the clerk of the peace for the time being, within every such county, shall sufficiently enroll and ingross in parchement the same deeds or writings indented as aforesaid; (7) and the rolls thereof at the end of every year shall deliver unto the said *Custos Rotulorum* of the same county for the time being, there to remain in the custody of the said *Custos Rotulorum* for the time being, amongst other records of every of the same counties where any such enrolment shall be so made, to the intent that every party that hath to do therewith, may resort and see the effect and tenor of every such writing so enrolled.

"II. Provided, always, That this Act, nor any thing therein contained extend to any manor, lands, tenements, or hereditaments, lying or being within any city, borough or town corporate within this realm, wherein the mayors, recorders, chamberlains, bailiffs or other officer or officers have authority, or have lawfully used to enroll any evidences, deeds or other writings within their precinct or limits; anything in this act contained to the contrary notwithstanding."

Sec. 68. Effect of the Statute of Enrollments on Conveyancing—Bargain and Sale Coupled with Lease and Release. The effect of the Statute of Enrollments was not to compel all grantees to make their holdings of the title a matter of record, although very probably that had been the purpose of its draftsmen. Its only effect was to change slightly the method of conveyancing. The Statute of Enrollments applied only where one person was *seised* to the use of another. The conveyancers completely avoided the effect of this statute by combining the bargain and sale with the ancient common law lease and release. The holder of a fee simple or of any freehold estate was said to be "seised," while the holder of an estate of less than freehold was not said to be "seised" of the land. A would now execute a bargain and sale of an estate of less than freehold to B. The consideration would raise a use in B, which would be executed by the Statute of Uses, giving B a legal estate of less than freehold which was not subject to the Statute of Enrollments. A would then execute a common law release to B, whereupon B had the fee simple title without any necessity of enrollment. Originally, the bargain and sale of the lease, and the release, were executed on successive days, but finally, the two were combined in a single instrument.

The same method was pursued in combining the covenant to stand seised with the release.

Sec. 69. Common Law Methods of Conveying Fee Simple Absolute in the United States—Feoffment with Livery of Seisin.[6] In the United States, feoffments with livery of seisin apparently never gained a foothold. Deeds have, to be sure, sometimes been construed as feoffments in order that they might be given effect but that construction did not make them feoffments. Singularly enough, in comparatively recent times, in the frontier sections of the United States, parties desirous of conveying land, frequently with no apparent knowledge of the early history of real property law, made their conveyances by means of the technique of feoffment and livery developed under similar conditions by their racial ancestors. There are numerous instances of conveyances of this type in the western states, which were executed prior to the establishment of a territorial status. In all of the states, however, at the present day, feoffment with livery of seisin has become merely a legal antiquity. Several factors have combined to produce this result. Early recording statutes (and recording was developed principally in the United States, beginning in Pennsylvania in 1682) provided that a grant, which of course is the same as a feoffment, should, when properly recorded, have the effect of a feoffment with livery of seisin. This is still the condition

---

[6] Bordwell, Seisin and Disseisin, (1921) 34 Harv. L. Rev. 726.

of the law in most of our jurisdictions. Feoffments with livery of seisin have not been abolished; they have simply been made unnecessary and as a result have practically disappeared. Other jurisdictions have expressly abolished feoffments with livery of seisin, substituting therefor some more convenient method of conveyancing.

Sec. 70. **Common Law Methods of Conveying Fee Simple Absolute in the United States—Exchange and Lease and Release.** The common law exchange transaction would apparently be available at the present day in the United States, but no evidence has been found indicating the use of this mode of conveyance anywhere in this country. The same thing is true of the common law conveyances by means of lease and release.

Sec. 71. **Methods of Conveying Fee Simple Absolute in the United States—Bargain and Sale.** The bargain and sale has been the most frequently used method of conveyancing in the United States. The words "bargain and sell" are generally used in a conveyance, even where the conveyance is being made under the form authorized by the statute providing that land may be transferred by simple forms of deeds. The determination of whether or not any particular conveyance operates under the Statute of Uses or under the local statute would be difficult and rather fruitless. It should be noted that a valuable consideration, either actual or expressed, is necessary if the conveyance is to be regarded as taking effect by way of bargain and sale.

Sec. 72. **Methods of Conveying Fee Simple Absolute in the United States—Covenant to Stand Seised.** So far as covenants to stand seised are concerned, they have been recognized in this country, but due to the fact that such conveyances can only be made to those standing in a close relationship by blood or marriage, their use has been rather infrequent. Even where the requisite "good" consideration exists, it is more usual to employ the method prescribed by the local statute or to convey by means of a bargain and sale, with a recitation of a pecuniary consideration.

Sec. 73. Statutory Methods of Conveying Fee Simple Absolute in the United States—Short Form Deeds. The establishment by statute of short form deeds might be thought to have resulted in their wide-spread use, which would have supplied the need of a convenient method of conveyancing, but in those communities which use title insurance, short form deeds are seldom used, and even in the communities where title companies have not yet gained a foothold, the natural tendency of the lawyer to make his craft in so far as possible a sacrosanct mystery has prevented any appreciable use of this most modern type of conveyance.

Sec. 74. Methods of Conveying Fee Simple Absolute in the United States—Quitclaim Deed. The release as a method of conveying a fee simple interest to which the grantor's title was imperfect found ready acceptance and frequent use in a country where, due to the claims of conflicting sovereigns, the condition of many early titles was highly speculative. The obvious advantage of employing that type of conveyance was that the grantor could not be accused of shady dealings, since by his very grant he recognized the dubious condition of his title. This method of conveyance is usually called a "quitclaim deed" in the United States, the name coming from one of the verbs used in the conveyance of release. Modern statutes have in many jurisdictions destroyed the original utility of this type of conveyance by inserting statutory covenants or warranties which make the conveyance practically the same in its effect as a feoffment with livery of seisin. There has been very little litigation construing these statutes so that at present the condition of a release or quitclaim deed in many jurisdictions is not at all clear.

Sec. 75. Devolution of Fee Simple Absolute on Death at Common Law—Inheritance. At early common law, as has been stated above, on a conveyance to A and his heirs the heir or expectant heir had an interest in the land by virtue of the grant (see sec. 52) and on the death of A the first taker, the heir or heirs took by purchase and not by descent, so that in the first instance there was no problem of inheritance. Even during that early period, however, on the death of the first taker's heir or heirs, the entire problem became one of inheritance, since by no possible stretch of the imagination could the heirs of the heirs of A, the first taker, be considered objects of the grantor's bounty. The rule that the heirs of the first taker took by descent and not by purchase, the evolution of which has already been discussed, did not then create a new problem. It simply moved an old problem one step forward.

From this time on, at common law, on the death of the holder of an estate in fee simple, the question immediately arose—who takes the property? The surviving spouse would take some interest, the history and development of which is stated elsewhere in this work,[7] and that interest was not conceived of as being an interest by descent. It arose merely from the marital status and was dependent on rules entirely separate from the rules of descent, and peculiar to the status. With the portion of the decedent's estate in fee simple controlled by those rules arising from the marital status we are not at present concerned. The problem of inheritance is concerned solely with the devolution of the rest of the decedent's fee simple interest.

The common law had a long and involved set of rules governing the descent of estates in fee simple held by one of the free tenures. Briefly, those rules were as follows:

A. Inheritances, in the first instance, never lineally ascended, but always descended to the issue of the person last seised, *in infinitum*. A man's legal heirs were those who were directly descended from him. Glanvil, writing towards the close of the twelfth century, stated [8] that a man could not be both heir and lord. In the case where A had granted land to his son B, and B, by doing homage, had recognized A as his lord, A was regarded thenceforth as being entitled to the services due from the land, and B to the land itself. Since A was entitled to the services, it was felt that he could not be allowed to take the land by inheritance from B. Only in the

---

[7] See sec. 108, post.
[8] Glanvil, VII, 1.

event that all of B's heirs died out, would A be entitled to the land, and then not as an heir of B, but through the operation of the principle of escheat. The importance ascribed to seisin, or the possession protected by the real actions, gave rise to the principle that only the person last seised of the land could be a "stock of descent," that is, that such a person was the one from whom descent must be traced in order to inherit the land.

B. The second common law rule of descent was that male issue were always preferred to female. That rule was applied, not only in the first instance in the descending line, but also when, on a failure of direct descendants, collateral relatives were admitted to the inheritance.

C. The third common law rule governing descent was that where there were two or more males in equal degree, that is, standing in the same degree of relationship to the deceased, only the eldest inherited, but where there were two or more females in equal degree, they took as co-heiresses. The rule of primogeniture was first applied to lands held by tenure by knight service, where it was clearly to the advantage of the lord to have the land descend as a whole to the person who was most likely to be able to perform the military services, that is, to the eldest son. The same reason did not apply where on his death a man left only daughters. When the incidents of tenure had come to be more important to the lords than the military services, they found it desirable to take homage from each daughter and thereby place themselves in the position of being entitled to the benefits of the tenurial incidents from each daughter's share of the land. In that way it came about that each daughter's claim was recognized. Originally those principles applied only to lands held by knight service, but by the end of the thirteenth century, they had been extended to include lands held by any one of the free tenures.

D. The fourth common law rule was that the lineal descendants *ad infinitum* of any deceased person represented, that is, stood in the same position as, their ancestor. That rule was fully recognized by the end of the thirteenth century, and enabled the children, male or female of the elder son, to take before the younger son.

E. The fifth rule of the common law regulating descent was that on the failure of the lineal descendants of the person last seised, the collateral relatives who were of the blood of the first purchaser, that is, of the person who had first brought the land into the family by some means other than descent, inherited. This rule was subject to the second, third and fourth rules stated above. A man's collateral relatives were those who, although not descended directly from him, were the descendants of one from whom he also descended. One person was said to be of the blood of another either if he had descended from him, or if he had descended from a common ancestor. Brothers and sisters of the whole blood, that is, those whose parents were the same couple, were of the blood of each other, but brothers and sisters, who had only one parent in common, were said to be of the half-blood, and were not considered as being of the blood of each other. It may be added that the husband and wife were not of the blood of each other.

F. The sixth common law rule of descent was that the collateral heir of the person last seised of the land must have been his collateral relative of the whole blood. Relatives of the half-blood could not, at common law, inherit from each other. This rule was the consequence of the rule that the one who was to inherit the land must be the heir of the person last seised and of the blood of the first purchaser. Obviously, if the common father had been the person last seised of the land, the half-brother could succeed to him on the death of the half-brother. However, if the son had been the person last seised, his half-brother could not succeed to him, because of the fact that he was not a relative of the whole blood although he was of the blood of the first purchaser. The sister of the whole blood succeeded to the brother of the whole blood. The land would sooner escheat, however, than that half-blood should succeed to half-blood.

G. The final common law rule governing descent was that in collateral inheritances, male stocks were preferred to female, unless the lands in question had in fact descended from a female. If land had descended from the father, then the ascent was traced in his line; if it had come from the mother, then the ascent was traced in her line.

Sec. 76. Devolution of Fee Simple Absolute on Death in the United States—Inheritance. In the Colonies, the common law rules of inheritance operated in their full rigor. It was generally felt, however, that those rules were not appropriate to the condition of a people who had broken away from the homeland to avoid the very institutions which that set of rules of inheritance tended to foster. The change from the old rules of inheritance was, however, a very gradual process. It started in some of the states long before the Revolution, but the first quarter of the nineteenth century had closed before it could be said that the American states had broken entirely from the common law scheme of inheritance.

A. As to the first common law rule, that inheritances lineally descended to the issue of the person last seised, *in infinitum,* but never lineally ascended, that rule has been universally changed in this country. Frequently the statute provides that, in certain cases, the decedent's property shall pass, on his death, to his mother or father. The provision found in some states is that if the deceased, on his death intestate, leaves no descendants, his father, or his father and mother, or his mother, shall inherit, together with his brothers and sisters. In some states, brothers and sisters are preferred to either of the parents. In the majority of the states, descent is now traced from the person last entitled to the land, regardless of whether he was the person last seised and regardless of his method of acquisition of the land, whether by descent or by purchase.

B. As to the second common law rule that gave priority to the male before the female descendants, that rule has been altered in all of the American jurisdictions, and at the present time all those who stand in the same degree of relationship to the deceased, whether male or female, share equally in the inheritance.

C. The third common law rule giving priority to the eldest of males related to the deceased in the same degree has also been altered in all of the states. All those in the same degree take equal shares of the inheritance.

D. As to the fourth common law rule that the lineal descendants *ad infinitum* of any deceased person represent their ancestor, the rule in all of the states is that the land descends to all the legitimate children of the decedent, who are living at his death, and to the descendants of any deceased children, those descendants taking *per stirpes* and not *per capita,* that is, the descendants of each child taking the share that their ancestor would have taken had he been alive, regardless of the number of descendants of each deceased child. If all of the children of the decedent are dead, on his death, the grandchildren of the decedent and the issue of deceased grandchildren inherit in their place. Where such descendants are not all in the same degree of relationship to the decedent, for instance, where some are grandchildren and others are great grandchildren, they inherit *per stirpes*. If all of the descendants are of the same degree of relationship to the decedent, in some states they take *per capita,* and in others *per stirpes*.

E. The fifth common law rule that on the failure of the lineal descendants of the person last seised his collateral relatives inherited, has been altered in the states. As stated above, it is no longer the rule that only the person last seised can constitute a stock of descent. In the United States, in the event that the decedent leaves no surviving issue and the statute does not provide that the realty pass entirely to the surviving spouse or to one or both of the parents, it descends among the collateral relatives of the deceased. In general, as between collateral relatives not specifically mentioned by the local statute, those who stand in an equal degree of relationship to the decedent take to the exclusion of those standing in a more distant degree of relationship to the deceased.

F. As to the sixth common law rule that the collateral kinsman who was to take must have been of the whole blood of the deceased, in the United States that rule has been changed in most jurisdictions, but the statutes differ widely. In practically all of the states, descent is traced from the one last entitled to the land, regardless of how he acquired it.

G. The final common law rule concerning collateral inheritance no longer exists in the United States, since in this country a male and a female standing in the same degree of relationship to the decedent share the inheritance equally.

Sec. 77. Devolution of Fee Simple Absolute on Death at Common Law—Devisability. As has been mentioned previously, all landholding originally was simply for the life of the first taker. There was no possibility then of control of the disposition of the property after death. After landholding had become inheritable, it was still very much to the interest of the lord to withhold all power of disposition of land by will. Such disposition would have defeated the most valuable rights of the lord, viz., the incidents of relief, wardship and marriage. Except in a few localities, where wills were permitted by a local custom, wills devising land, which had been known in Saxon times prior to the Conquest, were held to be invalid from the twelfth century.

Sec. 78. Development of Uses. It must be remembered that the Church was extremely powerful throughout the Middle Ages. It maintained its own courts and claimed jurisdiction over everything which by the broadest stretch of the imagination could be considered as pertaining to the spiritual side of life. Consequently it was possible to control the disposition of personal property after death by means of a testament which would be executed by the ecclesiastical court,— the Church of course by its very extension of this privilege usually benefiting by the terms of the testament. In the ecclesiastical courts a new method arose which, while it did not permit a man to make a will disposing of real property, nevertheless gave him all of the advantages of such a disposition. The holder of an estate in fee simple would, by a common law conveyance, alienate the estate to some trustworthy person who was instructed to hold the land to the use of certain persons or to the use of the grantor or to the uses to be indicated in the grantor's testament. By disposing of the use, the owner of the estate could then control the disposition of the property after his death, although in contemplation of the law he was not controlling the disposition of the land itself. Indeed, in contemplation of the law, he was no longer recognized as owning the land, his conveyee having succeeded to his title. Since the law no longer recognized his relation to the land, the temporal courts would not of course enforce the uses. So far as they were concerned, the uses did not exist.

The conveyee, however, was bound in conscience to recognize the uses. This made his conduct with reference to such uses a spiritual matter, and the ecclesiastical courts would enforce the uses. They could not enforce them by imprisonment or by a judgment, but they had at hand the interdict and excommunication, both very potent means of execution in a period in which belief in the everlasting fires of hell was universal.

About the fourteenth century, a new officer began to be heard of. The king had always had a chaplain, necessarily a cleric, who had gradually assumed the duties of the king's almoner. As the universality of the belief in an orthodox hell declined, holders of uses which were being disregarded began to petition the king's almoner, called the Chancellor, for assistance. The Chancellor, being a cleric, believed in the obligations of conscience which would normally have been enforced in the ecclesiastical courts. Being an officer of the king, he did not have to rely upon eternal punishment deferred until the after-life. He had temporal torture and temporal dungeons at his command, and he provided a most effective method of compelling the person who held the legal title, usually known as the trustee, to honor the uses. It might seem peculiar that the king, technically the chief of the group interested in preventing the control of property after death, would permit his confidential officer to behave in this fashion. This practice grew up, however, in the tumultuous period from the thirteenth to the sixteenth century. The king's interest was no longer identical with that of the other lords. He was in the process of becoming the head of all authority and consequently anything which would be disadvantageous to his tenants *in capite,* as this course of conduct obviously was, would be advantageous to him.

Sec. 79. Statute of Wills. In the reign of Henry VIII, four centuries of uses, with some acquisition of land by the Church on each transaction, had created in the Church itself a landowner much too influential, controlling far too great an extent of the realm for the comfort of a king as strong as Henry. His conflict with the Church over his divorce from Katherine of Aragon, and his execution of Sir Thomas More brought the situation to a head, and as a result the Statute of Uses was enacted in 1535, the effect of which so far as we are concerned at present was to abolish the device of the use to control the disposition of property after death. This was not the prime purpose of the statute, however, and due to the clamor aroused by its passage, the Statute of Wills was enacted five years later. That statute read:[9]

> "Where the King's most royal Majesty in all the time of his most gracious and noble reign hath ever been a merciful, loving, benevolent and most gracious Sovereign Lord, unto all and singular his loving and obedient subjects, and by many times past hath not only showed and imparted to them generally by his many, often, and beneficial pardons heretofore by authority of his parliament granted, but also by divers other ways and means, many great and ample grants and benignities, in such wise as all his said subjects been most bounden to the uttermost of all their powers and graces by them received of God, to render and give unto his Majesty their most humble reverence and obedient thanks and services, with their daily and continual prayer to Almighty God for the continual

---

[9] 32 Henry VIII, c. 1. Whereby a Man May Devise Two Parts of his Land (1540). The Act of Wills, Wards, and Primer Seisins.

preservation of his most royal estate in most kingly
honour and prosperity; yet always his Majesty, being
replete and endowed by God with grace, goodness, and
liberality, most tenderly considering that his said obe-
dient and loving subjects cannot use or exercise themselves according to their estates, degrees, faculties,
and qualities, or to bear themselves in such wise, as
that they may conveniently keep and maintain their
hospitalities and families, nor the good education and
bringing up of their lawful generations, which in this
realm (laud be to God) is in all parts very great and
abundant, but that in manner of necessity, as by daily
experience is manifested and known, they shall not be
able of their proper goods, chattels and other movable
substance to discharge their debts, and after their
degrees set forth to advance their children and posteri-
ties; wherefore our said Sovereign Lord, most virtu-
ously considering the mortality that is to every person
at God's will and pleasure most common and uncertain,
of his most blessed disposition and liberality, being
willing to relieve and help his said subjects in their
said necessities and debility, is contented and pleased
that it be ordained and enacted by authority of this
present Parliament, in manner and form, as hereafter
followeth; that is to say, That all and every person
and persons, having, or which hereafter shall have, any
manors, lands, tenements, or hereditaments, holden in
socage, or of the nature of socage tenure, and not
having any manors, lands, tenements, or hereditaments,
holden of the King our Sovereign Lord by knight-service, by socage tenure in chief, or of the nature of socage
tenure in chief, nor of any other person or persons by
knight-service, from the twentieth day of July in the
year of our Lord MDXL, shall have full and free lib-
erty, power, and authority to give, dispose, will, and
devise, as well by his last will and testament in writing, or otherwise by any act or acts lawfully executed
in his life, all his said manors, lands, tenements, or
hereditaments, or any of them, at his free will and
pleasure; any law, statute, or other thing heretofore
had, made or used, to the contrary notwithstanding."

The next section provided that the same power of devising the whole where a person held lands of the king by socage in chief, and also held lands of others in socage tenure, and had no land held by tenure by knight service should be extended to such persons.

The third section of the Act read:

"3. Saving alway and reserving to the King our Sovereign Lord, his heirs and successors, all his right, title and interest of *primer seisin* and reliefs, and also all other rights and duties for tenures in socage, or of the nature of socage tenure in chief, as heretofore hath ben used and accustomed, the same manors, lands, tenements or hereditaments, to be taken, had, and sued out of and from the hands of his Highness, his heirs and successors, by the person or persons to whom any such manors, lands, tenements or hereditaments shall be disposed, willed, or devised, in such and like manner and form, as hath been used by any heir or heirs before the making of this statute; and saving and reserving also fines for alienations of such manors, lands, tenements, or hereditaments holden of the King our Sovereign Lord in socage, or of the nature of socage tenure in chief, whereof there shall be any alteration of freehold or inheritance, made by will or otherwise, as is aforesaid.

"4. And it is further enacted by the authority aforesaid, that all and singular person and persons having any manors, lands, tenements, or hereditaments of estate of inheritance holden of the King's Highness in chief by knight-service, or of the nature of knight service in chief, from the said twentieth day of July, shall have full power and authority, by his last will, by writing, or otherwise, by any act or acts lawfully executed in his life, to give, dispose, will or assign two parts of the same manors, lands, tenements, or hereditaments, in three parts to be divided, or else as much of the said manors, lands, tenements or hereditaments as shall extend or amount to the yearly value of two parts of the same in three parts to be divided, in certainty and by special divisions as it may be known in severalty to and for the advancement of his wife, preferment of his children, and payment of his debts or otherwise at his will and pleasure; any law, statute, custom or other thing to the contrary thereof notwithstanding.

"5. Saving and reserving to the King our Sovereign Lord the custody, wardship and *primer seisin,* or any of them as the case shall require, of as much of the same manors, lands, tenements, or hereditaments as shall amount and extend to the full and clear yearly value of the third part thereof without any diminution, dower, fraud, covin, charge or abridgment of any of the same third part or of the full profits thereof."

The sixth section of the statute provided for the saving of fines on alienation. Other sections extended the power of devising land in all cases to two-thirds of lands held by knight service, and to the whole of those held in socage. The wardship of the king was reserved as to the third part of the lands held by knight service.

Thus, in substance, the Statute of Wills allowed landowners to dispose by will of all land held as an estate in fee simple by tenure in socage, and of two-thirds of their land held as an estate in fee simple by knight service. By making careful provision for the saving of primer seisins, reliefs and fines on alienation in the case of land held by socage tenure, and of the incident of wardship over the third part of the lands held by knight service, in favor of the king and other lords, the statute was designed to please everyone. The right to control the disposition of property after death was openly extended and at the same time the disadvantages to the lords consequent on such disposition were removed.

Land held by copyhold tenure did not come within the operation of the Statute of Wills, but in the sixteenth century a custom had become general to allow a copyholder to surrender his land to the use of his will.

Sec. 80. Statute of Tenures. When in 1660, by the Statute of Tenures, tenure by knight service was converted into tenure by free and common socage, the power to devise extended to the whole of the lands of which formerly only two-thirds had been devisable. The Statute of Tenures also abolished the remaining feudal incidents of both tenures, so that now for the first time since the passage of the Statute of Uses land was freely devisable.

Sec. 81. Devolution of Fee Simple Absolute on Death in the United States—Devisability. The colonists in the New World had been accustomed to the power of disposition of land by will, in some form or degree, for about a century before coming to this country. In some of the earlier statutes of the Colonies, the holder of real property was not given complete power over the disposition of property after his death, but was required to leave a certain portion of his estate intact for those who would normally be his dependents. In all of the Colonies, however, it was possible to make a will controlling the disposition of property after death. At the present day, every state has a statute controlling such disposition. In practically every state, however, there is some limitation on the amount of property which can be so devised. It has been considered sound social policy to prevent a testator from disinheriting certain persons who should be the natural objects of his bounty and throwing them on their own devices and the public. The nature of such limitations will be discussed in the section dealing with Life Estates.

b. *Qualified Fee Simple*

Sec. 82. Qualified Fee Simple Estate. The estates in fee simple which we have been discussing up to this point are the normal type of fee simple estate, usually denominated fee simple absolute. In addition to such fees simple absolute, the common law recognized estates in fee simple which were qualified in either one of two ways. One type was called a fee simple subject to a special limitation or a determinable fee simple. The other type was called a conditional fee simple, or a fee simple subject to a condition subsequent. Very early in the history of estates in land, grantors started to create estates which were fees simple so long as they lasted, and which could conceivably endure until the failure of the heirs of the grantee just as in all other estates in fee simple, but which could be terminated earlier upon the happening of some specified event. This type of estate certainly existed prior to the enactment of the Statute of Quia Emptores in 1290, and that it has been a vigorous and constant form of interest is evidenced by the frequency with which it was noticed by the early writers such as Bracton, who wrote about the middle of the thirteenth century, and Littleton, who wrote toward the end of the fifteenth century.

The first thing to be noticed with reference to these qualified estates in fee simple is that in creating them at common law the magic words "and his heirs" were essential because, after all, these interests were fundamentally estates in fee simple.

Sec. 83. Qualified Fee Simple Estate—Varieties—Fee Simple Subject to a Special Limitation (Determinable Fee Simple). The method of stating the event upon which the estate may terminate prior to the death of the holder of the estate leaving no heirs whatsoever is the determining factor as between the two types of qualified fees simple.

A fee simple subject to a special limitation (determinable fee simple), is an estate in which in creating the interest the grantor, in addition to stating that the interest is to the grantee and his heirs, in some way indicates that the duration of the estate depends upon the concurrence of collateral circumstances. An early example given by Blackstone [10] is the case of a grant "to A and his heirs, tenants of the manor of Dale." Common modern examples are: "To A and his heirs so long as the property is used for the conducting of religious services"; "To X School and its assigns so long as the Darwinian theory is taught in the school"; "To A and his heirs so long as oil and gas are produced on the premises." It is

---

[10] 2 Bl. Comm. c. VII * 109.

to be noted that in all of these examples the additional words limiting the durability of the interest, called words of special limitation, are words giving the sense of duration until the occurrence of an event, or so long as a certain state of affairs exists. On the happening of that named event, or on the cessation of that specified state of affairs, the interest of the then holder automatically terminates, and the property is said to "revert" to the grantor or to his heirs, if he be dead. The interest of the grantor or of his heirs is termed a "possibility of reverter."

Sec. 84. **Qualified Fee Simple Estate—Fee Simple Subject to a Condition Subsequent (Fee Simple Conditional).** This is an estate in which in creating the interest, the grantor in addition to stating that the interest is to the grantee and his heirs, in some way indicates that the grantor and his heirs reserve the power of terminating the interest on the occurrence of some collateral event. It is to be noticed that there is a considerable difference between this interest and the fee simple subject to a special limitation. The form of words in an estate of the latter type indicates continuity of the interest until the happening of the event. In a fee simple on condition subsequent, the words indicate continuity until the happening of the event, but termination then only at the option of the grantor or of his heirs, if he be dead. Examples of grants creating estates in fee simple on conditions subsequent are: "To A and his heirs forever, but if spirituous liquor shall ever be sold on the premises, the estate to revert to the grantor and his heirs"; "To A and his heirs forever provided that on his failure to operate a grist mill on the premises, the grantor and his heirs may re-enter." The words commonly used in creating a determinable fee simple are "until," "so long as," "while" and "during"; in creating a fee simple on condition subsequent "provided that" or "on condition that."

Both of these forms of qualified fees simple were used very commonly from the earliest times in the history of the land law. However, in 1831, a conveyancer named Saunders, writing on the subject of Uses and Trusts, stated it to be his opinion that the Statute of Quia Emptores had made the creation of both of these types of qualified estates in fee simple impossible. Despite his position, the English courts continued to recognize such interests with no difficulty.

Sec. 85. Qualified Fee Simple Estate in the United States. In the United States qualified fee simple estates have always been extremely common. It is obvious that interests of this type serve a very useful economic purpose. The grantor who gives land to a church or to an educational institution as well as the grantor with decided views on temperance has found both forms of qualified fee simple estates ready tools to his hand. Although he cannot affirmatively control the use of the property, since the holder of a fee simple is immune from all control over his conduct with reference to the property save that of organized society, he can, by giving the property in one of these forms, negatively control the conduct of the donees by assuring them at the time of the gift, that on failure to comply with his ideas, the property will either revert automatically or can be retaken by him or his heirs.

Throughout the American history of real property law, there was no doubt as to the power to create these interests until the last decade of the nineteenth century, when John Chipman Gray followed the "heresy" of Saunders. Again, despite the opinion of that very eminent scholar of the law, the courts continued to recognize qualified fee simple estates. The point is still discussed in legal periodicals, but so far as the courts are concerned, such discussion is academic in the strongest sense of that word.

In those jurisdictions having a minority group, which is socially unrecognized, grantors have attempted to use the qualified fee simple estate to prevent lands from being alienated to a member of such a group. These experiments have not been signally successful, since the courts, in the exercise of their normal liberalizing tendency to keep the land freely alienable, have usually declared such limitations or conditions invalid as opposed to public policy. In some jurisdictions (and those are the only ones in which the question would really be important), this has been evaded by placing the limitation or condition not upon the alienation to a member of the race or group considered socially undesirable, but upon the occupancy or possession by a member of such a race or group. Other courts have upheld the restraint against alienation to such persons so long as the limitation or condition was for a limited period only.

Sec. 86. **Qualified Fee Simple Estate—Conveyances.** What has already been said in reference to the *inter vivos* transfer of an estate in fee simple absolute applies also to the fee simple determinable, but for the fact that the estate conveyed is still subject to the possibility of reverter, and also to the fee simple on condition subsequent, but for the fact that the estate conveyed is subject to the same power of termination on the part of the grantor or his heirs, upon breach of the condition.

Sec. 87. **Qualified Fee Simple Estate—Devolution on Death.** On the intestate death of the owner of an estate in determinable fee simple such estate passes in accordance with the principles of intestate succession already discussed as applicable to an estate in fee simple absolute, but all interests so passing are still subject to the possibility of reverter. Likewise on the death of the holder of an estate in fee simple on condition subsequent, the interest passes in the same manner as an estate in fee simple absolute, but the interest so passing is still subject to the power of termination on the part of the grantor or his heirs, on the breach of the condition. Both the owner of an estate in fee simple determinable and the owner of an estate in fee simple subject to a condition subsequent can devise their interests, but the interest of the first type so passing is still subject to the possibility of reverter, and that of the latter type to the power of termination.

c. Maritagium

Sec. 88. **The Maritagium at Common Law.** Shortly after the Conquest, a new species of estate or interest called the *maritagium* appeared in the land law. This was a marriage portion, usually given to a woman by some close relative; the motive of the donor was not only to provide for the woman herself but for any children she might bear while married. In order to effectuate this purpose, the donor stated that the gift was "to M and the heirs of her body." Since the donor, who had an estate in fee simple descendible to all of his heirs, was granting an estate which would descend only to the grantee's direct heirs, some interest was left in him. Consequently should the direct heirs of M fail at any time, the land would revert whence it came, that is, to the donor.

By the year 1200, the maritagium had developed into a very popular form of grant. It was no longer restricted in its use to females and their issue, but was the method of conveyance used by any individual who was granting land to a relative and desired that land to remain in the family. The disfavor with which the courts regarded anything tending to prevent the free alienability of land led them to circumvent the donor's intention to benefit the children of the first taker by holding that a gift to A and the heirs of his body created a conditional fee.

d. Conditional Fee

Sec. 89. Conditional Fee at Common Law. This was a peculiar type of interest in which, immediately after the execution of the grant, the grantee took an interest the extent of which would not be determined until a later time. The extent of the interest was conditional on the birth of a child to the grantee. If no child were born to him, he enjoyed the estate only during his own life; at his death it reverted to the grantor. Of course under these circumstances, an alienation, regardless of how much the first taker purported to grant, was effective in transferring to the alienee only the interest that the first taker had, so that on the death of the first taker the original grantor could recover the land from the alienee. If, however, a child were born, the interest of the first taker was immediately converted into a conditional fee simple. This interest was not a complete fee simple because on the death of the first taker the interest would pass only to his lineal heirs. In all other respects, however, it was an estate in fee simple. If, after the birth of issue, the first taker alienated the property, the alienee took an estate in fee simple absolute. The alienee's estate was thus good against any claim by the direct heirs of the first taker as well as against any claim by the original grantor or his heirs. The failure of the issue of the first taker had no effect upon the interest of the alienee.

The result of these constructions was the further linking of the "three black professions." Occasionally, in old books, one finds pictures of a child-birth, with the physician, the priest and the scrivener in attendance, the physician to deliver the child, the priest to baptize it, and the lawyer to deprive it of its birthright by assisting the father in the execution of a conveyance passing an estate in fee simple.

Sec. 90. Conditional Fee in the United States.[11] In only four states in this country are conditional fees recognized at the present time. Those states are Iowa, Nebraska, Oregon and South Carolina. Their existence is possible in those states due to the fact that the Statute De Donis Conditionalibus, which we will consider in a moment, is not in force in those jurisdictions.

Sec. 91. Statute De Donis Conditionalibus. The construction as a conditional fee of a gift to a donee and the heirs of his body clearly circumvented the purpose of the original grantor and naturally aroused considerable discontent on the part of the powerful landowning class that dominated the Legislature. As a result, in 1285, to remedy this condition, they passed the famous Statute De Donis Conditionalibus, the effective portions of which are as follows: [12]

> "First, concerning lands that many times are given upon condition, that is, to wit, where any giveth his land to any man and his wife, and to the heirs begotten of the bodies of the same man and his wife, with such

---

[11] American Law Institute, Restatement of Property. Proposed Final Draft, pp. 195-196, p. 213.

[12] Statute of Westminster II, 13 Edward I, c. 1. De Donis Conditionalibus (1285).

condition expressed that if the same man and his wife die without heir of their bodies between them begotten, the land so given shall revert to the giver or his heir; in case also where one giveth lands in free marriage, which gift hath a condition annexed, though it be not expressed in the deed of gift, which is this, that if the husband and wife die without heirs of their bodies begotten, the land so given shall revert to the giver or his heir; in case also where one giveth land to another and the heirs of his body issuing, it seemed very hard and yet seemeth to the givers and their heirs, that their will being expressed in the gift was not heretofore nor yet is observed. In all the cases aforesaid after issue begotten and born between them, to whom the lands were given under such condition, heretofore such feoffees had power to aliene the land so given, and to disinherit their issue of the land, contrary to the minds of the givers, and contrary to the form expressed in the gift; and further, when the issue of such feoffee is failing, the land so given ought to return to the giver or his heir by form of gift expressed in the deed though the issue, if any were, had died; yet by the deed and feoffment of them to whom land was so given upon condition, the donors have heretofore been barred of their reversion of the same tenements which was directly repugnant to the form of the gift: wherefore our lord the king, perceiving how necessary and expedient it should be to provide remedy in the aforesaid cases, hath ordained, that the will of the giver according to the form in the deed of gift manifestly expressed shall be from henceforth observed, so that they to whom the land was given under such condition shall have no power to aliene the land so given, but that it shall remain unto the issue of them to whom it was given after their death, or shall revert unto the giver or his heirs if issue fail, either by reason that there is no issue at all, or if any issue be, it fail by death, the heir of such issue failing. . . . And forasmuch as in a new case new remedy must be provided, this manner of writ shall be granted to the party that will purchase it: 'Command A. that justly, &c., he render to B. the manor of F. with its appurtenances, which C. gave to such a man, and such a woman, and to the heirs of the said man and woman issuing'; or, 'which C. gave to such a man in free marriage with such a woman, and which, after the death of the aforesaid man and woman, to the aforesaid B., son of the aforesaid man and woman, ought to descend, by the form of the gift aforesaid, as he saith'; or, 'which C. gave to such a one and the heirs of his body issuing, and which after the death of the said such a one, to the aforesaid B., son of the aforesaid such a one, ought to descend, by the form, &c.' The writ whereby the giver shall recover when issue faileth is common enough in the Chancery. And it is to wit that this statute shall hold place touching alienation of land contrary to the form of the gift hereafter to be made, and shall not extend to gifts made before. And if a fine be levied hereafter upon such lands it shall be void in the law, neither shall the heirs or such as the reversion belongeth unto, though they be of full age, within England, and out of prison, need to make their claim."

e. Fee Tail

Sec. 92. Estate in Fee Tail. The language of the statute is quite clear. As a result of it, the conditional fee could no longer be created, and a return was made to the construction of the early maritagium. It appeared under a new name, however, and was henceforth known as the estate in fee tail, so called from the Latin word *talliatum* and the French word *taillé,* being regarded as an estate whose descent was cut down or limited to the heirs of the body of the donee. The statute provided that the land should descend *forma doni,* that is, according to the terms of the gift and that the donee should have no power to deprive either his own heirs or the grantor and his heirs of what was rightfully theirs under the terms of the gift. The holder of the estate in fee tail could still alienate, but the alienation did not create a fee simple interest in the grantee. Such alienee took only an estate for the life of the holder of the estate in fee tail, and the heirs of that holder of the estate in fee tail, or the heirs of the grantor, if there were no direct descendants of the holder of the estate tail, could enforce their rights by legal action. The writs by which these rights were enforced were created by the statute, and were called writs of *formedon, (per formam doni,* according to the terms of the gift). They were further particularized by the type of interest which was being protected, as *formedon in descender,* available to the lineal heirs of the first taker, and *formedon in reversion,* available to the original grantor or his heirs, direct or collateral.

Sec. 93. Estate in Fee Tail—Interest of the Holder. Very shortly after the passage of the Statute De Donis, the question arose whether or not an heir of the first donee in tail had a broader power of alienation or only the same power of alienation as that of the first taker. It was finally held that each successive direct descendant of the first taker on receiving the estate in fee tail had only the same power of alienation as the first taker had had. Each could alienate an estate which could be enjoyed only for the duration of his own life. The holder of an estate in fee tail then had an interest much more restricted than that of the holder of an estate in fee simple. He could enjoy the land, and do with it what he wished, but he was subject to control not only by the State acting on behalf of society in general but also by his presumptive heirs and the grantor and his heirs, each of whom had substantial interests to which the law accorded protection. Thus the sum total of his rights, privileges, powers and immunities was considerably less than that of the holder of an estate in fee simple.

Sec. 94. Estate in Fee Tail—Creation. Following the passage of the Statute De Donis, it was held that an estate in fee tail was created whenever in the grant, words had been used which prior to the statute would have created a conditional fee of one of the types mentioned in the statute. There was thus greater latitude of expression in creating an estate in fee tail than there was in creating an estate in fee simple. The magic words "and his heirs" were also required, but the addition of any form of words limiting the heirs to those pro-created by the grantee would create an estate in fee tail. The common form was "to A and the heirs of his body."

Sec. 95. Estate in Fee Tail—Varieties. There were four classes of estates in fee tail: 1. The estate in fee tail general. Here the limitation was to a person and any heirs of his body. 2. The estate in fee tail special. Here the limitation was to a person and the heirs of his body by a particular spouse. 3. The estate in fee tail male. Here the limitation was to a person and the heirs male of his body. 4. The estate in fee tail female. Here the limitation was to a person and the heirs female of his body.

Of course it was possible to combine class one with class three or with class four, and class two with class three or with class four. For example, a grant to A and the heirs male of his body created an estate in fee tail male general, while a grant to A and the heirs female of his body by his wife B created an estate in fee tail special female. In the estate in fee tail special, there was the possibility of an interest arising which could not arise in an estate in fee tail general. Where the spouse named in the grant died without leaving issue surviving, the donee would have an estate for his life which could not conceivably descend. He was then known as the "tenant in tail after the possibility of issue extinct."

Sec. 96. Estate in Fee Tail in the United States.[13] In the United States, except in those states in which the Statute De Donis was not in force, it was apparently possible to create estates in fee tail in the earliest period of our history. From the beginning, however, it was felt that the estate in fee tail was completely out of harmony with our institutions. The early settlers were, in the main, not members of the great landholding families in the lands from which they had come, and were not desirous of creating on the soil of the new land the conditions from which they had fled. Early in the Colonial period, legislators started to change the estate in fee tail. The

---

[13] American Law Institute, Restatement of Property. Proposed Final Draft, pp. 196-206, 221.

field has been prolific of legislation, and as a result of a series of statutes in the various states, and in one instance a provision in the State Constitution,[14] it can be stated definitely that at the present time an estate tail is recognized in only six states. Those states are Delaware, Kansas, Maine, Massachusetts, Rhode Island (as to deeds only), and Wyoming. Estates in fee tail formerly existed in Maryland, New Jersey, New York, North Carolina, Pennsylvania, and Virginia. There is an additional group of states composed of Idaho, Louisiana, Nevada, Oregon, Utah, and Washington, in which the question has never been definitely settled by legislation or by litigation. The statutes in the remaining states fall into three groups:

A. States wherein a limitation formerly sufficient to create an estate in fee tail now creates either a fee simple absolute in the first taker, or a fee simple in the first taker subject to reverting back to the grantor if the first taker dies unsurvived by descendants. There are twenty-four states in this group: Alabama, Arizona, California, District of Columbia, Georgia, Indiana, Kentucky, Maryland, Michigan, Minnesota, Mississippi, Montana, New Hampshire, New Jersey, New York, North Carolina, North Dakota, Oklahoma, Pennsylvania, South Dakota, Tennessee, Virginia, West Virginia, and Wisconsin.

B. States wherein a limitation formerly sufficient to create an estate in fee tail now confers a life estate on the first taker, the heir of the first taker receiving a fee simple absolute. There are seven states in this group: Arkansas, Colorado, Georgia (limited to certain types of conveyance), Illinois, Missouri, New Mexico, and Vermont.

C. States wherein a limitation formerly sufficient to create an estate in fee tail now creates an estate in fee tail for the lifetime of the first taker, the heir of such first taker re-

---

[14] Texas Constitution (1845) art. 1, sec. 26. The authors, however, are convinced that this provision applied not to the estate tail as known in English law, but to the *mayorazgo,* a form of estate tail in Spanish law with which the draftsmen of that constitution were much more familiar.

ceiving an estate in fee simple absolute. This group is composed of three states: Connecticut, Ohio, and Rhode Island.

Sec. 97. Estate in Fee Tail—Conveyances at Common Law. Since after the passage of the Statute De Donis, the holder of an estate in fee tail had substantially only an estate for his own life, and could convey no greater interest than that, the methods of coveyancing used were those applicable to the normal life estate, which will be considered in the discussion of that estate.[15]

Sec. 98. The Courts Circumvent the Statute De Donis. The legislative victory of the landholding group was an extremely hollow one. The courts still had their ready weapon, construction, and in a series of constructions within a comparatively short time managed to evade the restrictions imposed upon the estate in fee tail by the Statute De Donis, just as an earlier generation of judges had done with the original maritagium. The device used in this instance obviously could not be a bare construction of the limitation, however. That had already been done, and the legislative branch of the government had overruled it. It was necessary for the courts therefore to find a new device in which their real purpose would not be so patent. This new method, which evolved only gradually, was the one used so frequently by the courts of common law—a fiction. Fictitious legal proceedings, known as fines and common recoveries, were the means used to evade the irksome restrictions imposed upon the estate in fee tail as a consequence of the Statute De Donis.

Sec. 99. The Common Recovery. The common recovery was an action already in existence, used normally for another purpose. The machinery of this action was made efficacious for this purpose by its combination with the doctrine of warranty. Where the grant of an estate of inheritance was accompanied by a warranty, which is a legally enforceable promise, the donor, or warrantor, was bound to protect the possession of his donee. The result of this was that if someone

---

[15] See secs. 114 and 117, post.

ousted the donee by establishing a superior title to the land, the donor was obliged to give the donee or his representative lands of equal value. The heirs of the donor were bound by the burden of the donor's warranty, whereas the heirs of the donee were entitled to its benefits. Early in the reign of Edward II, towards the close of the thirteenth century, it was held that, unless the heir of the tenant in tail had received from the tenant in tail by descent assets of equal value to the lands which the tenant in tail had alienated with a warranty, he was not bound by that warranty. The courts utilized a fiction to effect that result. The recovery, combined with the warranty, operated thus. If A had granted lands to B and his heirs, binding himself and his heirs to warrant B's title, and thereafter X claimed the land from B, B "vouched A to warranty," that is, called upon him to fulfill his obligation of warranting the title. In the event of X's being successful in establishing his claim, judgment was given that X recover the land from B, and that A, the warrantor, convey to B lands of equal value. This was applied to estates in fee tail as follows: X, a friend of B, the tenant in tail, claimed the land granted to B by A for an estate in fee simple, by bringing a writ of right. B, instead of vouching A to warranty, vouched to warranty a straw man, Y, who admitted his duty to warrant. X and Y thus became the nominal plaintiff and defendant. Y then asked the court for "leave to imparl," that is, to talk the matter over out of court with X. Y did not return to the courtroom after this conference which placed him in contempt of court, and consequently X was given judgment by default that he recover the land from B for an estate in fee simple. B was given a judgment against Y, ordering Y to convey to B lands of equal value. X immediately conveyed the fee simple estate to B. Y, of course, was unable to satisfy the judgment against him in favor of B, but of this fact the law never takes cognizance. Since all of the persons interested in the entailed lands would have been compensated had Y actually been able to satisfy the judgment by conveying to B lands of equal value and since the judgment was compensation so far as the law was concerned, the recovery barred all those interested in the conveyed lands. In a later period, the various steps were simply enrolled on the court records, and the court crier commonly played the part of the straw man, Y, being known as the "common vouchee." Sir Frederick Pollock phrased [16] the situation happily when he declared that the crier of the Court of Common Pleas "thus passed his life cheerfully and not ungainfully in perpetual contempt of the Court of Common Pleas and liability to be fined at the king's discretion."

During the greater part of the Middle Ages, the common recovery was considered a collusive proceeding rather than a regular mode of conveyance and it was only because the use of a recovery, in combination with the doctrine of warranty, coincided with the policy of the court in favor of free alienability of land, that it was allowed to operate as a conveyance.

Sec. 100. The Fine. The other fictitious suit made use of to avoid the restrictions imposed by the Statute De Donis was the fine. The fine received its name from the Latin words, *finalis concordia,* a compromise that brought an end to the action. The suit was one brought by an intended alienee against an intended alienor, as the result of a prior agreement between the two. With the court's permission, the action was then compromised, by the defendant agreeing upon terms with the claimant and then abandoning his defense. Thereupon the whole transaction was enrolled of record, a document known in later times as the foot or chirograph or indenture of the fine being drawn up. Since the fine was enrolled, incontestable evidence of the transaction was thus afforded, and a guarantee was also furnished against forgery. There was the further aspect that a party to a fine was obliged to respect its terms, since if he infringed them, an action lay against him, and he could be imprisoned. Moreover, the fine set a short preclusive term, finally fixed at five years, running against the whole world, parties, privies, and strangers.

The fine had been in use for a long time prior to the enactment of the Statute De Donis, and it will be recalled that one

---

[16] Pollock, The Land Laws (1923), 84.

of the provisions of that statute was that a fine should have no effect upon the estate in fee tail. However, once the common recovery was allowed to be used as a method of barring the entail, the reason for the prohibition of the use of the fine ceased. By statute of Henry VII and Henry VIII, therefore, the fine was allowed to bar the issue of the tenant in tail, but not the grantee or his heirs, the reversioners.

Sec. 101. Effects of Fine and Common Recovery Contrasted. The interest taken by the person in whose favor a fine was levied was therefore like an estate in fee simple in that it descended to his heirs generally. It was, however, unlike an estate in fee simple in that if the issue of the tenant in tail failed, the grantor or his heirs could defeat the estate of the alienee. The type of estate held by the alienee was known as a "base fee." The recovery alone completely barred the entail, by cutting off the right not only of the issue of the tenant in tail, but also of the reversioners.

Sec. 102. Barring the Entail in the United States. Due to the wide spread belief already noted that estates in fee tail were not suited to the conditions of the New World, the colonies early enacted statutes enabling the holder of an estate in fee tail to bar the entail without the formality of a fine or common recovery. The method adopted was some type of simple conveyance although sometimes there is an additional requirement of publicity, such as delivery in open court, and usually an express recital in the conveyance of the purpose of the grantor, viz., to bar the entail, is necessary.

Sec. 103. The Fine in the United States.[17] These disentailing conveyances, however, lacked some of the advantages of fines and recoveries, so despite the possibility of using such conveyances, fines or common recoveries were occasionally resorted to in some of the states. The use of fines seems to have been limited to New York, and was abolished there in 1829.

---

[17] American Law Institute, Restatement of Property. Tentative Draft Number 2, pp. 89-90. Bordwell, Seisin and Disseisin, (1921) 34 Harv. L. Rev. 726.

Sec. 104. The Common Recovery in the United States.[18]
Common recoveries were popular, especially in Pennsylvania, where their use is apparently still possible, although there is no indication in the appellate courts of that state of their use within the last seventy-five years. Recoveries are still said to be permitted by the statutes of Delaware. In practice, however, fines and common recoveries have been completely replaced by conveyances by deeds. Some of the states authorizing disentailing deeds retain the restriction originating in the procedure of fines and recoveries that only one who has a possessory estate in fee tail, or one who is joined in the conveyance by the person who has the prior possessory estate of freehold can make such a disentailing.

Sec. 105. Estate in Fee Tail—Devolution on Death at Common Law—Inheritance. Of course, in the estate in fee tail, the form of the gift determined the devolution of the estate. In the case of an estate in fee tail general, only the heirs of the body of the tenant could take, that is, only lineal heirs, collateral heirs being excluded by virtue of the terms of the gift. In the case of the estate in fee tail special, only those who were the lineal heirs of the named husband and wife could inherit. In the case of the estate in fee tail male, the lineal male heirs alone could take. For example, if the donee in tail male had a daughter who died, leaving a son, that grandson could not inherit the estate in tail male for he could not trace his descent wholly through the male line. Conversely, in the case of an estate in fee tail female, if a man died leaving a son, who left a daughter on his death, that granddaughter could not inherit the estate. In the case of a man who had two estates in tail, one in tail male and the other in tail female, if the tenant in tail died survived by a daughter who left a son on her death, the grandson could succeed to neither of the estates. Obviously, he could not inherit the estate limited to heirs female, nor could he inherit the estate in tail male, since he traced descent through a female.

---

[18] American Law Institute, Restatement of Property. Tentative Draft Number 2, pp. 89-90. Bordwell, op. cit. supra.

Sec. 106. Estate in Fee Tail—Devolution on Death at Common Law—Devisability. As stated in the preceding discussion on the alienation of an estate in fee tail, since the original taker of the estate and each of his successors in interest held the estate only for his own life, he had nothing that could be devised.

Of course, in any situation in which the entail has been barred, the estate has become an estate in fee simple and the rules of descent, applicable to an estate in fee simple, control. In the various states in this country, where a conveyance which would have created an estate in fee tail at the common law, now, due to a statute, creates either an estate in fee simple or some variety of interests culminating in an estate in fee simple, the rules of descent governing an estate in fee simple are applicable.

f. Life Estates

Sec. 107. Life Estates. The final estate classified as a freehold interest was the life estate. As we have already mentioned, originally all land was apparently held only for the life of the first taker. A grant to A with no words of limitation, that is, "to A," gave A only an interest for his life; the grantor would be bound only by what he had said and what he had said was "to A." Consequently the interest granted could exist only so long as A. This continued to be the construction placed upon any grant in which there were no words of limitation, and, in later times, upon any limitation, the form of which was peculiar or unknown to the law, for example, "to A so long as he shall live in Albert Lea."

Life estates are usually classified into legal and conventional life estates. The legal life estates are those which arise by operation of the law. The conventional life estates are those which are created by act of the parties.

Sec. 108. Legal Life Estates at Common Law.

(a) Tenancy in Tail After the Possibility of Issue Extinct. As has been noted previously, where a person held a fee tail

special, and the named spouse died without leaving issue surviving, the holder of the estate, known as the tenant in tail
after the possibility of issue extinct, had an interest which
endured only for his life.

(b) Dower. Dower was an interest given to the wife for
her maintenance after the death of her husband. It consisted
of a life estate in one-third of all the lands of which her husband had, at any time during the existence of the marriage,
been seised. There was no necessity that issue be born in
order that dower might attach. It was only necessary that the
husband be seised of an inheritable estate, that is, of an estate
in fee simple or in fee tail.

(c) Curtesy. Curtesy was the interest given to the husband in the lands of the wife, after her death. It was not the
exact counterpart of dower, since it attached not merely to
one-third, but to all of the lands. It attached only to lands
as to which the wife had died seised of an inheritable estate.
In addition, in order for curtesy to attach it was essential
that a child capable of inheriting the land be borne alive during
the marriage. For example, if the wife were seised of an
estate in tail female, a son were born, and then the wife
died, the husband would not have an estate by curtesy because the child was incapable of inheriting the land.

(d) Estate Iure Uxoris. Strictly speaking, this was not
an estate at all although it is commonly spoken of as an
estate. At common law, a married woman was conclusively
considered incapable of management of her own affairs. Consequently, the husband had a very great power of control over
all of her property, both real and personal. So far as her real
property was concerned, the husband, simply by virtue of the
marriage, *iure uxoris,* (by right of the marriage) held a
freehold interest which could endure until the death of the
survivor. It was a true life estate.

Sec. 109. Conventional Life Estates at Common Law.

(a) Life Estate for the Life of the Taker. This is the
common form of life estate of which we spoke at the beginning of this section. The durability of the estate is meas-

ured by the life of the taker, as it is in the legal life estates, but the estate is created not by operation of law but by the form of the conveyance e.g. "to A for life" or "to A" (by deed).

(b) Estate Pur Autre Vie (For the Life of Another). This is a life estate in which the durability is measured not by the life of the taker, but by the life of some other person. It is always created by the conveyance between the parties— not by operation of law. An example of this is a grant to A for the life of B, or if A, the holder of an estate for his own life, conveyed to X, this would create in X an estate *pur autre vie*—for the life of A.

Sec. 110. Life Estates—Interest of the Holder. All of these life estates despite the variety in the modes of their creation and in the measurement of their durability conferred upon the holders of the estates the same rights, privileges, powers and immunities. In very early times, when the life estate was far more common than the estate in fee simple, the tenant for life was free to use and abuse the property as he saw fit. In 1278 the Statute of Gloucester changed this by providing a remedy for those entitled to the land after the life estate against a life tenant who abused the property. This remedy was called a "writ of waste," and since that time improper conduct on the part of the life tenant has been called waste. The statute provided for forfeiture of the thing wasted, plus triple damages. Waste was defined as damage caused by the voluntary act of the life tenant, but a reasonable use of timber for firewood and repairs, (called *"botes"* and *"estovers"*) did not constitute waste.

Save for this disability imposed to protect those who would follow him on the land, the tenant for life in his use of the land was in the position of the holder of an estate in fee simple. He was subject to no more control on the part of organized society or third persons than was the holder of an estate in fee simple, but his privileges were restricted by his responsibility to the person who would be entitled after his death, to whom he was obliged to deliver the land in substantially the same condition as it had been when he received it, exclusive of normal wear and tear. In general, the life tenant was also required to pay the ordinary taxes on the land, to keep the property in repair and to pay assessments for benefits which would probably not endure longer than his life estate.

Sec. 111. Life Estates Subject to a Condition or Special Limitation. It should be noted that conventional life estates could also be created subject to conditions or special limitations identical with those before considered applicable to fees simple determinable and conditional fees. Common usages of this type would be: "To W so long as she remains a widow," and "To M for life, but if she should remarry, the heirs of the grantor may re-enter."

Sec. 112. Legal Life Estates in the United States. We have already noted in our discussion of the estate in fee simple, that the words "and his heirs" are no longer required to create an estate in fee simple in many of the states. Consequently, grants which would at common law have created a life estate because of the lack of words of limitation will, in this country, at the present day, convey whatever interest the grantor had. There has been no change, however, in the construction placed upon a grant in which the form of limitation is peculiar or unknown to the law.

(a) Tenancy in Tail After the Possibility of Issue Extinct. The statutes making impossible the creation of an estate in fee tail in most jurisdictions have of course necessarily disposed of this interest. In those jurisdictions which permit the creation of estates in fee tail or in which there are existent estates of that type, created prior to the enactment of such statutes, this type of life estate still exists.

(b) Dower. In the United States, there is always some provision for the support or maintenance of the wife after the death of her husband. The common law concept of dower, however, has been changed everywhere. In those states which have a community property system, the wife's interest in the community property has supplanted the dower provision. In

all of the other states, there is some type of provision by means of which the widow receives a portion of all the lands of which her husband was seised during the marriage, the extent of which varies in accordance with the number of children. She usually does not receive the interest for life, however, but in fee simple.

The husband, of course, has a power of disposing by will of all property of which he dies seised. In most jurisdictions the widow has an election; she can take either the portion given to her by statute in lieu of dower or the provision made for her by the will. Usually in taking the statutory portion, she is regarded as taking by descent, being referred to as a "forced heir." In a few jurisdictions this portion is regarded in the nature of a dower estate rather than an estate by descent.

(c) Curtesy. In most jurisdictions in the United States, curtesy has been abolished by statute, and the widower has been made a "forced heir," usually taking in the same proportion and in the same way as the widow.

(d) Estate Iure Uxoris. The conditions which had given rise to the common law estate *iure uxoris* were originally existent also in the United States. There were, however, three general waves of legislation which radically altered the condition of married women before the law. The earliest group of statutes, enacted in the first quarter of the nineteenth century, made possible the creation of separate estates at law for married women, estates over which their husbands had no control. The next group of statutes, passed in the middle of the nineteenth century, gave control over the property to the married women themselves. These are the most important for our purposes. The final group of statutes, enacted at the end of the nineteenth century, relieved married women of practically all of their remaining disabilities having to do with contractual powers. As a result of these statutes, the husband has no control over the wife's property save, in most jurisdictions, the purely negative power of refusing to

validate her conveyance by joinder. There is then no estate *iure uxoris* at the present day.

Sec. 113. Conventional Life Estates in the United States. These estates exist in the United States in the same form as at common law in England.

Sec. 114. Life Estates—Conveyances at Common Law. Since the estate for life was a freehold interest held by freehold tenure, the modes of conveyance discussed under Estates in Fee Simple Absolute, were applicable. That is, the conveyance could take the form of a feoffment, accompanied by livery of seisin, or the deed of exchange, plus entry. A deed of surrender could also be used where the life tenant wished to give up his term to the person entitled after his death. The transaction could probably be accomplished in an informal manner without deed or other ceremony, but deeds of surrender were by no means uncommon. Of course the lease and release, the bargain and sale, and the covenant to stand seised, which arose after the passage of the Statute of Uses, as modes of conveying estates in fee simple, were also available for the conveying of life estates. Writing was necessary, after the passage of the Statute of Frauds, in 1677, in any of these forms of conveyance. The fine and common recovery could also be used as methods of transferring the life estate.

Sec. 115. Interest Created in Alienee by Conveyance by Life Tenant. When the holder of a life estate conveyed, all that he was capable of granting to another was an estate which would endure for his own life. Consequently, the normal conveyance by a life tenant created in his grantee an estate *pur autre vie*. He could also create an estate less than his own, and since every freehold interest was considered greater than any non-freehold interest, he could convey a term for years of any length, subject to termination upon his own death before the expiration of that period.

Sec. 116. Tortious Conveyance by Life Tenant. There is another situation peculiar to the alienation of a life estate. If a life tenant, by a conveyance which did not operate under the Statute of Uses but by virtue of transmutation of possession by one of the common law conveyances which passed seisin, (feoffment with livery of seisin, fine, common recovery or exchange) purported to convey to the grantee a greater interest than he actually had, which would necessarily have been either an estate in fee simple or in fee tail, since only those two interests were greater than a life estate, the mere form of the conveyance invested the feoffee with seisin, tortious to be sure, but still seisin. This transaction would have several consequences, which will be considered in other connections. For our present purposes, we must notice the effect of that tortious conveyance upon the life estate. Since the life tenant owed homage and fealty to his grantor, an attempt to convey an interest which would be opposed to his grantor's wishes "smacked of treason." It was a denial of his lord's right and constituted a negation of the very essence of homage. Such conduct could not go unpunished and the punishment took the form of the forfeiture of his estate.

Sec. 117. Life Estates—Conveyances in the United States. The changes in the methods of conveying an estate in fee simple which have already been considered in the sections dealing with the estate in fee simple, apply also to the conveying of life estates in the United States. In connection with forfeiture, it should be noted that the common law methods of conveyancing which transferred seisin were little used in the early period of American history and have since become obsolete. Consequently, forfeiture at the present day is an extremely rare phenomenon, since most of our conveyances are effective either under the Statute of Uses or modern conveyancing statutes, and since in a great many of our states it is expressly provided by statute that a grantor can convey only the interest which he holds in the property. There is evidence of an occasional use of a deed of feoffment with livery of seisin [19] or of a common recovery [20] for the express

---

[19] McElwee v. Wheeler, 10 S.C. 392 (1878); Faber v. Police, 10 S.C. 376 (1878); Redfern v. Middleton's Executors, Rice 459 (S.C. 1839); Dehon v. Redfern, Dudley's Eq. R. 115 (S.C. 1837).

[20] Waddell v. Rattew, 5 Rawle 231 (Pa. 1835); Stump v. Findlay,

purpose of forfeiting a life estate. This is possible, however, in only a few jurisdictions and has not occurred even in those jurisdictions within recent years.

Sec. 118. Life Estates—Devolution on Death of Life Tenant at Common Law—Estate Pur Autre Vie. From the very nature of the interest of the holder of a legal life estate or a conventional life estate for the life of the taker, it is obvious that no question of inheritance could arise, since the interest terminated on the death of the holder. An estate *pur autre vie,* however, could raise the problem of inheritance, if the holder died prior to the death of the person by whose life the duration of the estate was measured; for example, a grant by X to A for the life of B, where A died while B was still living. Since the estate *pur autre vie* was not considered one of inheritance, the heirs of A could not take by descent, and since they were not mentioned in the grant, could not take by purchase. A's personal representatives could not take since they took only personal property and an estate *pur autre vie,* being a freehold interest, was real property. X could not properly take since he had disposed of an interest which by its terms was not to return to him until B's death, by whose life the duration of the estate was measured and B was still living. Under those circumstances, the law returned to the atavism of occupancy, and the first person who entered could hold the land until the termination of the estate by B's death. Such a taker was spoken of as a "general occupant."

Somewhat later in the development of the law, it became common for the grantor of any estate *pur autre vie* to grant it to the first taker and his heirs, for instance, "to A and his heirs for the life of B." In this type of grant, if A predeceased B, the interest was inherited by his heir, who would hold until the termination of the interest by B's death. The heir was then spoken of as a "special occupant."

2 Rawle 167 (1828) (Here the court held the life estate was forfeited even though the recovery itself was void for technical reasons of pleading). Abbott v. Jenkins, 10 S. & R. 296 (Pa. 1823); Lyle v. Richards, 9 S. & R. 322 (Pa. 1823); Dunwoodie v. Reed, 3 S. & R. 435 (Pa. 1817).

Sec. 119. Life Estates—Devolution on Death of Life Tenant in the United States—Estate Pur Autre Vie.[21] In the United States, in many jurisdictions, there are statutes dealing with the matter of devolution of the estate *pur autre vie*, on the grantee's death. Some of those statutes provide that the undevised residue of such an estate shall pass to the heirs as realty; others provide that such residue shall pass to the personal representatives as personalty. In general, the statutes make no provision for special occupancy. Where there is no statutory provision concerning special occupancy, and the statutory provision in the jurisdiction is to the effect that the residue of the estate shall pass as personalty, the right of special occupancy should probably not be given to the grantee's heirs, even where the estate had been given to the grantee and his heirs. Likewise, even where the limitation is to the grantee "and his heirs," if the statutory provision is that the residue of the estate shall pass to the heir, the heir will probably take, not as special occupant, but by descent. The right of the special occupant is, however, recognized by statute in two states, Maryland and South Carolina, and where the limitation is also "to the heirs," in Pennsylvania.

It is possible that special occupancy might be recognized in those jurisdictions which have no statute on the subject, in case the grant was to the grantee and his heirs. No adjudications have been found on that point, however. Where the limitation is simply to the grantee, it is probable that the residue of the estate would be regarded as within the statute providing for the descent of real property, with no attention being given to the fact that the estate is not technically one of inheritance.

II. Non-Freehold Estates—Varieties

Sec. 120. Non-Freehold Estates—Varieties. So far our discussion has been concerned solely with freehold estates,

---

[21] Tiffany, Herbert, The Law of Real Property (2d ed. 1929), Vol. I, sec. 35, pp. 94-95.

which in early times were the only interests recognized as estate in land. There were, in addition, estates termed non-freehold interests. The basic distinction between the freeholds and the non-freeholds was that the freehold was an estate in land, that is, a collection of multital or *in rem* rights, privileges, powers and immunities with reference to the land, available against all the world, but the non-freehold was a collection of paucital or *in personam* rights, privileges, powers, and immunities with reference to the land, available only against some particular or determinate person or persons. The non-freehold estate was, then, originally a mere contractual interest as opposed to an estate in land.

The distinguishing characteristic of the non-freehold interests from their earliest recognition to the present day has been that the estate is sure to come to an end on the lapse of some specified time, however remote that time may be. The duration of a freehold estate is uncertain—based on the longevity of an individual or individuals, or on the eventual dying out of a line of heirs. The duration of a non-freehold estate is certain—the lapse of a period of days or years is known.

The non-freehold estates were classified according to the period of potential duration as follows: term for years, tenancy at will, periodic tenancy or tenancy from year to year, and tenancy at sufferance.

a. Term for Years

Sec. 121. Term for Years—Nature of the Interest. The term for years is the basic type of non-freehold. It is an interest granted for a definite period. The period is not necessarily a year or more, and in that sense the designation of the interest is a misnomer. It may be a day, a month, or a thousand years, but in each of these instances there is some definite limitation of the duration which is known at the time of the creation of the interest, and regardless of the length of that duration the interest is called a term for years. The border line interest of this type is a term for a definite period (usually quite long e.g. 999 years) where the lessor covenants to renew the lease perpetually. This is still a term for years, however, because at any given moment the time when the present term will expire is known.

Sec. 122. Term for Years—Creation of the Interest at Common Law. Just as we saw in the creation of a fee simple at the earliest period, no written instrument was necessary in creating a term for years. The proper method of creating an estate for years was to use the words "let and demise," stating the duration of the interest, followed by an entry on the part of the lessee. After the passage of the Statute of Frauds in 1677 it was necessary to create a term for years in writing if the term was to endure for a longer period than three years, but even after this statute a shorter term could be created merely by an oral transaction followed by entry. The minimum legal requirement, however, was not the measure of normal practice. As will be seen shortly, since the lessee's interest was merely contractual, if the lessor and the lessee were to be able to enforce their agreement by an action of covenant, there must be some method of proving it. In consequence a written lease was the common method of creating a term for years from the earliest period.

Whether the term was created orally or by writing either prior to or subsequent to the Statute of Frauds, however, the letting itself did not create the term for years. Until the words of demise had been followed by the lessee's actual entry upon the land, his interest was not complete. Until entry the lessee had merely a right to enter upon the land in reliance on his contractual rights called an *"interesse termini."*

Sec. 123. Term for Years—Creation Subject to a Condition Subsequent or a Special Limitation. A term for years can be, and frequently is, created subject to a special limitation or condition. The modern law of landlord and tenant abounds with examples, familiar to everyone, of terms of this type. The modern apartment or dwelling house lease for example usually contains one section fairly bristling with conditions against noise, obstructing common passages, keeping animals in the dwelling and so forth. Here, the provisions are usually conditions subsequent, leaving the lessor the option as to whether he prefers the tenant or the annoyance. Modern commercial leases usually contain provisions that on an assignment for the benefit of creditors, or an act of bankruptcy the term will end. Here the provision is a limitation since an automatic termination is to the advantage of the lessor. Since the courts have never carried their insistence on free alienability to terms for years the lessor can subject the term to any condition or limitation that he sees fit.

Sec. 124. **Term for Years—Position of the Tenant for Years—Remedies—Rise of Ejectment.** Terms for years were originally not considered interests in the land. They were based not upon the feudal concept of status, but rather upon a mere contractual relationship between the grantor and the grantee. Until the end of the twelfth century, the tenant for years, or termor, could be evicted by the lessor or by a third person, and there was no remedy by means of which he could regain the land. In comparison with the freeholder, the rights, privileges, powers and immunities of the tenant for years were very limited. He could use and enjoy the land since he was on it, but there was no real protection against those who interfered with him in his enjoyment of the land. Due to the existence of the contractual right, if the tenant for years were ejected by the lessor, he could bring an action on the contract and might possibly recover a judgment for the return of the same land, if his term had not expired. If he had been ejected by a stranger, his action against the lessor on the covenant would result in a judgment that land of equivalent value be assigned to him. He could not proceed against the stranger who had ejected him. The remedy for that wrong was vested in the lessor, since the wrong was one against the seisin and only the lessor had seisin.

In the first half of the thirteenth century, a new action was made available to the tenant for years, called *"quare ejecit infra terminum."* This action could be used, however, only against a person claiming under the lessor. About the end of the reign of Henry III, during the third quarter of the thirteenth century, the tenant for years also acquired the right of bringing an action of trespass q.c.f. *(quare clausum fregit)* against all persons unconnected with the lessor who interfered with his possession. By this action damages alone could be recovered. As new writs continued to arise from the action of trespass, a special writ was created for the benefit of the termor. This was the writ of *"trespass de ejectione firmae"* (ejectment). It was available against all who interfered with his privilege of exclusive possession and enjoyment of the land. He could originally recover only damages by this writ, but just at the close of the Middle Ages in 1499, it was decided that he could also, in this action, recover possession of the land. As pointed out by Holdsworth,[22] the reasons for this change were in the main economic. The decay of the labor-service system had resulted in a great extension of the practice of letting land to tenants for years. Obviously damages alone afforded such lessees entirely inadequate compensation. The government also wished to stop the depopulation of the rural districts caused by the conversion of arable land into pasture for sheep, and to continue to enforce the rule that the ejected lessee could not regain the land would have facilitated the operations of landlords who were pursuing that policy.

When we have reached this point, the protection accorded by the law to the tenant for years is scarcely less than the protection accorded to the holder of a freehold interest. In fact, the termor's new remedy was so efficient compared with the older remedies available to holders of freehold estates, that eventually the freeholder devised a means of rendering the termor's remedy available to him.

Sec. 125. Term for Years—Position of the Tenant for Years—Obligations—Waste. In the preceding section we concerned ourselves exclusively with the remedies which were

---

[22] Holdsworth, An Historical Introduction to the Land Law (1927), pp. 72-73.

gradually extended to the tenant for years as against the lessor and those claiming under him, and as against third persons not connected with the lessor. We must now consider the obligations of the tenant for years. In the earliest time, it would seem that although the tenant for years had practically no legal remedies, on the other hand, there were practically no legal remedies against him. The first change in this condition was the extension of the writ of Prohibition to cover a case where the tenant for years was engaged in conduct which would result in a diminution of the value of the land. However, a more definite rule was needed, and after two prior attempts it was finally provided by the Statute of Gloucester (1278) which provided for an action commenced by a writ of Waste by the lessor against the lessee in this situation. The statute provided that the tenant would lose the thing wasted and would be required to pay triple damages. It was early decided that the tenant was liable only for "voluntary waste," and the defense that it had been accidental or an Act of God was a good defense. By the time of Coke (reign of Elizabeth) it had been decided that a tenant for years was also liable for "permissive waste," that is a diminution in value occasioned by omissions to act on the part of the tenant. Later decisions, however, made this much more doubtful. It was decided quite early that a tenant for years could not be held liable for "ameliorative waste," that is a change in the condition of the premises which is really an increase in value, unless it was an injury from the point of view of the lessor.

The growth of the remedies for conduct deemed waste created one of the basic concepts applicable to an estate for years. At the expiration of the term, the land must be returned to the lessor in about the same condition as it was when the tenant for years received it, exclusive of normal wear and tear.

Sec. 126. Term for Years—Position of the Tenant for Years—Doctrine of Fixtures—Trade Fixtures Exception. There are two other limitations upon the interest of the termor, which must be considered in order to complete the picture of his interest. The common law had by this time developed in other connections a doctrine that anything firmly affixed to the land became a part of the land, under the name of a "fixture." An exception was made to the doctrine in favor of the tenant for years. With reference to articles affixed to the land by him for use in his trade or business he was permitted to remove such articles so long as they were removed before the end of the term. Otherwise the normal rule would apply. This was spoken of as the trade fixtures exception to the doctrine of fixtures. It developed in the early sixteenth century.

Sec. 127. Term for Years—Position of the Tenant for Years—Emblements—Doctrine of "Waygoing Crops." In connection with land used for agricultural purposes, if a tenant for years planted a crop prior to the end of his term, which crop was still standing at the end of his term, the crop became the property of the lessor, because the tenant had planted it at a time when he knew that his term would not be sufficiently long to permit him to harvest the crop. In early law, in a few counties, a doctrine called the doctrine of "waygoing crops" prevailed, which permitted a tenant for years to harvest after the expiration of his term crops planted during the term, so long as they were of a certain type. The doctrine usually applied to winter grain crops.

Sec. 128. Term for Years—Conveyances at Common Law—Sublease—Assignment—Surrender. Once the term for years had been created, the tenant's interest could be alienated by him, either by sublease or by assignment. A sublease or underlease is where the termor makes a lease with another for a shorter term than he himself has. This necessarily means that he himself retains a part of his interest (a reversion). When the tenant for years grants his entire term to another, the grant is called an assignment. A deed of surrender, without livery of seisin, was available to the tenant for years who wished to transfer his interest to the person who was entitled after the termination of his estate.

Sec. 129. Term for Years—Creation of the Interest in the United States. As we have already mentioned, in England a term for less than three years could be created by an oral letting followed by entry, but a term for a period in excess of three years was required to be created by a writing. Technically the American states are said to have adopted the common law as of the fourth year of James I (1607), since that was the date of the first settlement. As to statutes enacted in England subsequent to that date their acceptance in this country required some special act of adoption. (It must be remembered that several of the American colonies were not founded until after the passage of the Statute of Frauds.) The English statute is in force in at least two of the jurisdictions of the United States. Every other jurisdiction has some form of Statute of Frauds, requiring a writing for the creation of a term for years. Usually a writing is required for any term in excess of one year.

Failure to comply with the provision of the Statute of Frauds will have a varying effect depending on the local statute. For instance under the English statute, the attempt to create a term in excess of three years without a writing is expressly stated to result in the creation of a tenancy at will. A great many of the American states provide for the same result. Another group makes the conveyance invalid without providing what its effect will be. Under this type of statute, it is probable that a tenancy at sufferance results.

It should be noted that where the statute provides that an abortive attempt to set up a term for years creates a tenancy at will, the payment and acceptance of rent on an annual basis will convert this into a tenancy from year to year.

It will be recalled that under the English law the oral letting, or the writing was not itself sufficient to create the term for years. There was an absolute necessity for entry by the lessee in order to create the term, and prior to such entry he was said to have only an *"interesse termini."* This problem has been raised only infrequently in the United States, but such authority as there is follows the common law position.

Sec. 130. Term for Years—Position of the Tenant for Years—Remedies and Obligations in the United States. By the time that the colonies were established, the peculiar form of trespass available to the termor, that is, the action of ejectment, had been in use for several centuries in England. This was also true of the action of trespass *quare clausum fregit* as against third persons. Both of these actions were used immediately in the colonies. From the very beginning then, in this country, the tenant for years had complete protection by these actions. There is no evidence that the older action *quare ejecit infra terminum,* or the action of covenant were ever used by the termor in the United States.

The liability of the tenant for voluntary waste (conduct which injures the reversion), permissive waste (failure to repair or maintain), and ameliorative waste (substantial change in the condition of the property even though it may be a benefit to the lessor) has been recognized in this country from the very beginning of our case law. In England the old action of waste had been replaced by an action on the case for waste prior to the establishment of the colonies, so that this was the normal common law action when we adopted the common law. The extent to which the Statute of Gloucester is in force in this country is a matter of considerable uncertainty, but most of the states have a local statute of similar import, and even where there is no applicable statute the action of trespass on the case for waste or the equivalent code action is available.

Sec. 131. Term for Years—Position of the Tenant for Years—Fixtures and Emblements in the United States. The concept of fixtures was adopted very early in the United States. Some few of the highly industrialized states have carried the concept beyond the common law basis and treat as fixtures not only all things attached to the realty, but also all equipment necessary to the operation of the industrial plant. This is known as the "assembled plant doctrine."

The trade fixtures exception appeared very early in the case law in this country. It has followed the English case authority very closely, even to the extent (in the majority of jurisdictions) of refusing to apply this exception to farming as a trade.

The concept of emblements, and the exception of "way-going crops" has been applied in this country throughout our legal history. Just as in its origins, the exception of "way-going crops" has been applied only to crops sowed in the fall for harvesting in the early summer. The most familiar example is winter wheat. A few of the western states have broken away from the basic idea of emblements in the English cases. The original distinction was that crops which had been severed from the land were personalty. Crops that were still standing were part of the realty. These western states have taken the position that the determining factor is not severance, but whether or not the crop is still drawing sustenance from the soil. The majority of jurisdictions, however, still follow the original idea.

Sec. 132. Term for Years—Conveyances in the United States—Sublease—Assignment—Release. The lease frequently contains a provision, inserted by the lessor, that the tenant may not sublease or assign without the consent in writing of the lessor. This policy is considered so important at the present day that many states have statutes invalidating any attempt to sublease or assign without the consent of the lessor. The practical importance is that if a tenant can sublease without such consent, he can turn the property over to an undesirable tenant, even though the original lessee remains liable for the rent. If the tenant can assign without such consent, he can not only place an undesirable tenant on the premises, but he can also avoid his own responsibility for the rent, giving the landlord in return the obligation of a person who may not necessarily be financially responsible.

The courts in this country take the same basic position as the English courts that a conveyance of the entire residue of the term is an assignment, but a conveyance of less than the entire residue of the term is a sublease. The difficulty arises where the lessee assigns the entire residue of the term but retains a right to re-enter for breach of a condition. The cases are in hopeless confusion as to whether such a transaction is a sublease or an assignment. There is a strong argument in favor of each conclusion, and the jurisdictions are about equally divided on the point, those holding it is an assignment taking the position that the right of entry retained by the original lessor is too slight an interest to be considered in this connection, those holding it is a sublease taking the position that the right of entry, even though not an estate is a substantial interest in land.

A conveyance by the tenant to the lessor is still spoken of as a surrender. The instrument used in the United States today is usually referred to as a quitclaim deed. In addition it is possible to have a release or surrender by operation of law.

b. Tenancy at Will

Sec. 133. Tenancy at Will—Nature of the Interest. The tenancy at will, although classified as a non-freehold interest lacks the distinguishing characteristic of those interests. It is not given for a definite term. It is a tenancy which may be terminated at the will of either the lessor or the lessee, and at common law no notice was required for such termination. Since the interest is so slight, as to be scarcely an estate at all it is not alienable, any attempt at alienation by the lessee being considered in law a manifestation of his will to terminate the relation. The relation is also terminated by the death of either the lessor or the lessee. Similarly the commission of waste by the lessee is considered a manifestation of his will to terminate.

Sec. 134. Tenancy at Will—Creation of the Interest at Common Law. The creation of this type of tenancy was subject to the same provisions as the term for years at common law. All that was required was a letting and an entry by the lessee. The Statute of Frauds did not change this by requiring a writing, since a tenancy at will is not an interest to endure for a greater period than three years. So far as the intentional creation of a tenancy at will was concerned, it was covered only by the old common law. With respect to the unintentional creation of tenancies at will however, the Statute of Frauds had a very important effect. The statute provided expressly that an attempt to create a term in excess of three years by parol would create merely a tenancy at will, so that from the passage of the statute (1677) on, unintentional creation of tenancies at will was fairly common.

Sec. 135. Tenancy at Will—Position of the Tenant at Will—Remedies. Due to the very nature of the interest, the problem of any action by the tenant against the lessor could not arise, since any conduct on the lessor's part which would have given rise to an action by a tenant for years, would, in a tenancy at will, be a manifestation of the will of the lessor that the tenancy was at an end.

As against third persons, presumably at the earliest period, the tenant at will would be in the same position as the tenant for years. He would have no action against third persons who disturbed his possession since all of the actions available at that time were predicated upon seisin and he did not have seisin. After the action of trespass *quare clausum fregit* arose, it is very probable that the tenant at will could bring this action against a third person who disturbed his possession. There seems to be no clear evidence on the point. This is probably due to the practical difficulty that would face a tenant at will in proving damages, making any action a pure luxury from which he could not expect compensation.

Sec. 136. Tenancy at Will—Position of the Tenant at Will—Obligations. The Statute of Gloucester, which went further than its predecessors on the question of waste, provided the new writ of Waste only against "him that holdeth by the law of England or otherwise for term of life, or for term of years or a woman in dower." This did not mean, however, that the tenant at will was free to commit waste. We have already noted that this was one method of terminating the interest—the commission of waste by the tenant was deemed in law a manifestation of his will to terminate the interest. In addition where the tenant at will committed voluntary waste, the lessor, from the time of Littleton (middle of the fourteenth century) could bring an action of trespass against him. It was a logical inconsistency to permit one out of possession, but seised, to use an action based entirely on possession, against one who admittedly had possession, but it arose out of the necessity of the situation.

Sec. 137. Tenancy at Will—Position of the Tenant at Will—Fixtures—Emblements. The normal concept of fixtures, that all things attached to the realty became realty and remained with the land at the end of the term applied also in the tenancy at will. The doctrine of trade fixtures was also applied however, and the tenant at will, where the tenancy terminated otherwise than through his fault, had a reasonable time after the termination of the tenancy to enter and remove his trade fixtures.

The law of emblements really arose in connection with this interest. In mediaeval times, all leases of agricultural land were tenancies at will. In order to curb rapacious landlords and foster application and energy on the part of all those working the land, the courts evolved the doctrine that where a tenant at will planted a crop and the tenancy was terminated by the lessor before the harvest, the tenant had free rights of egress and ingress not only to harvest, but also to cultivate the crop. The title to the growing crop remained in the tenant. The reason for this distinction in his favor was that when he planted the crop he had not known when his interest would terminate. If after planting the crop, the tenant terminated the tenancy at will, he did not get his emblements. The title to the crop went to the lessor, since there was no longer any reason for granting an exception from the normal rules.

Sec. 138. Tenancy at Will—Nature and Incidents of the Interest in the United States. Tenancy at will in the United States is, just as it was at common law, an extremely indefinite interest which may be terminated at the will of either the lessee or the lessor. Quite generally in the United States however, statutes require that the lessor give some notice (usually thirty days) to the lessee to terminate the interest.

Any manifestation of will by the tenant (or by the lessor where there is no requirement of notice) will terminate the interest, and the death of either party will automatically terminate it. In some jurisdictions the commission of waste is such a manifestation, just as at common law, but this position is by no means uniform in this country.

Intentional creation of a tenancy at will operates just as it did at common law. Unintentional creation of these tenancies, depends, of course, on the form of the local Statute of Frauds. About half of the states have statutes which operate as the English statute, creating a tenancy at will where, for any one of several reasons, there has not been strict compliance with the statute. In the other jurisdictions, noncompliance usually creates a tenancy at sufferance, not a tenancy at will. The remedies of the tenant at will in this country are in the same position that they were at common law.

In some jurisdictions the obligations of the tenant at will vary considerably from the common law position, however. Those jurisdictions which have the Statute of Gloucester, or a local statute modeled on it have, of course, no liability for waste, other than the trespassory action for voluntary waste; but in some few jurisdictions, the local statute on waste imposes the liability on "any tenant of land," or in itemizing the tenants, expressly names the tenant at will.

The doctrines of fixtures and emblements, with their exceptions, apply to tenants at will in the United States, just as they did at common law.

c. Tenancy from Year to Year—Periodic Tenancy

Sec. 139. Tenancy from Year to Year—Nature and Creation of the Interest at Common Law. The tenancy from year to year arose primarily because of the inconvenience of the tenancy at will. In early times, terms for years seem usually to have been for long periods. This new type of interest was a term which for each year was definite as to its termination and on the tenant's remaining in possession and the landlord's accepting an installment of rent, the term was automatically extended for another year. Gradually the same doctrine was applied to every situation in which the lessor evidenced his acquiescence in the tenant's holding over after the termination of the initial period. This created periodic tenancies which might be for month to month, week to week, year to year, or in fact for any period for which a term of years was given.

In creation and conveyance, terms from year to year, or periodic tenancies, partake of several natures. Since the tenancy from year to year was an outgrowth of the tenancy at will the same general rules apply for intentional creation. Merely words of letting or demise followed by entry created the interest. No written instrument was necessary unless the initial period (which would be the same as each subsequent period) was in excess of three years.

Unintentional creation arose in a peculiar fashion. The Statute of Frauds provided that an abortive attempt to create a term for a period in excess of three years would create a tenancy at will. The decisions built up the further doctrine that the payment and receipt of rent in such a situation would result in a periodic tenancy. If the rent was paid and received on an annual basis the resulting tenancy would be from year to year, if on a quarterly basis, from quarter to quarter, if on a monthly basis, from month to month.

The periodic renewal, since it was implied in law, was subject to no requirements and arose merely on the concurrence of the holding over by the tenant and the acquiescence by the lessor in that holding over.

So far as conveyance of the interest was concerned it partook, not of the nature of the tenancy at will, but of the nature of the term for years. Alienability was possible because at any given moment the remainder of the term was definite. All of the rules applicable to conveyance of a term for years were applied, including the concepts of sublease and assignment.

Sec. 140.   Tenancy from Year to Year—Position of the Tenant. Since as to each consecutive period the interest of the tenant from year to year was certain in its duration, he was placed in exactly the same position as the tenant for years. He had the same rights, privileges, powers and immunities, the same remedies and obligations, and the same rules as to fixtures and emblements, with the trade fixtures exception and the "waygoing crop" exception.

Sec. 141.   Tenancy from Year to Year in the United States. In some few of the American states the tenancy from year to year and all other periodic tenancies are regarded purely as tenancies at will, and all of the rules previously stated applicable to tenancies at will in this country operate. In the large majority of jurisdictions in this country, however, the periodic tenancy is regarded as much more akin to the term for years. It is at the very least a term for one definite period with the possibility of further terms for identical periods. It arises in the same way as at common law in a conveyance of a term abortive because of the provisions of the Statute of Frauds followed by the payment and receipt of rent on the basis of some period which establishes the nature of the periodic tenancy. Most jurisdictions have, in addition, a statute requiring the lessor to give notice to the tenant, of his desire to terminate their relationship some time in advance (usually ninety days) of the last day of the current period.

d.   Tenancy at Sufferance

Sec. 142.   Tenancy at Sufferance—Nature of the Interest at Common Law. A tenancy at sufferance is really not a tenancy at all but only a defense to an action of tort. It is not an interest in the land, but a mere personal privilege that the holder can assert as a defense to an action. It arises in any situation where a tenant obtains possession lawfully (e.g. by entry under a lease) but withholds possession wrongfully (e.g. by holding over after the term without the consent of the lessor). He cannot be treated as a trespasser since his original entry was lawful, and the lessor cannot bring ejectment without first making an entry, since ejectment is basically a trespassory action.

The law of trade fixtures and emblements does not apply since the tenant at sufferance has no interest in the land.

The only possible actions against the tenant at sufferance by the original lessor are ejectment to recover the premises, case for waste and case for mesne profits. He is liable in all three actions, but since they are all trespassory the lessor must first enter in order to bring them.

Sec. 143. Tenancy at Sufferance—Creation and Conveyance at Common Law. Since the tenant at sufferance had no estate in the land and the relationship arose by operation of law, there were no requirements as to its creation, and there was nothing that could be transferred to a third person by the tenant.

Sec. 144. Tenancy at Sufferance in the United States. The term tenancy at sufferance has received a slightly more extended usage in the United States than it had at common law. In addition to having the same meaning as it there had, it is in some jurisdictions applied to the interest which arises on the failure of an interest under the Statute of Frauds. These are the jurisdictions, mentioned above, which do not follow the English form of the statute and make no provision for the effect of a conveyance abortive under the statute.

Due to a misunderstanding of the meaning of "sufferance" in this sense, several state legislatures have enacted statutes requiring the lessor to give a certain period of notice (usually thirty days) to a tenant at sufferance before a summary action for eviction is available to him. To avoid the absurdity involved in such a requirement several of the courts have found it necessary to entirely twist the concept, so that some few jurisdictions will be found with case law taking the position that a tenant who enters rightfully and holds over wrongfully is not a tenant at sufferance unless there is a showing of laches on the part of the lessor.

e. Non-Freehold Interests—Devolution on Death

Sec. 145. Non-Freehold Interests—Devolution on Death at Common Law. The non-freehold interests could clearly not be considered real property in the full sense of the word, due to the fact that the holder of such an interest had no seisin. Thus early in the thirteenth century lawyers began to speak of a non-freehold interest as a chattel, but as a peculiar sort of chattel, called a chattel real. Consequently, the Church, in taking control of the devolution of a man's personal property on his death, also took control of his chattels real. Thus if a man died intestate leaving a non-freehold interest, that interest would descend not to his heirs under the rules of primogeniture, but to his "next-of-kin," a broader group favored by the canon law. If the term were limited to the tenant for years and his heirs, however, it would pass to the tenant's common law heir on his death intestate. This applied only to terms for years. The other interests were purely personal and terminated by the death of either lessor or lessee.

Sec. 146. Non-Freehold Interests—Devolution on Death in the United States. These matters had been settled and acquiesced in for a long period, in fact for more than a century, before our first reported cases in the United States. These cases show that in this country there was never any doubt in the minds of the judges that the term for years could be devised and gifts over could be created therein.

So far as intestate succession was concerned, the American statutes have retained the position of the common law. Non-freehold interests are chattels real, and although we have abolished the distinction between heirs and next-of-kin, the question is still important since personal property must be exhausted in the payment of debts before the real property of the decedent can be subjected to those debts. By our Wills Acts, personalty and real property alike can be disposed of by one instrument called either a will or a will and testament, but it is effectually only a single instrument and the administration of both personalty and realty is committed to the same court.

f. Rent in Non-Freehold Interests

Sec. 147. Rent in Non-Freehold Interests at Common Law and in the United States. In connection with non-freehold interests, for example, terms for years, we are accustomed to thinking of the rent as the most important element of the situation. It undoubtedly is the most important economic factor in the situation, but it does not arise by operation of law. The rent is set between the parties by the agreement expressed in the lease, and is set up in the lease as a covenant on the part of the lessee to pay the rent.

Rent really has two entirely different aspects. From the standpoint of the lessor, the rent is an incorporeal hereditament, like an easement of way, and can be divided, apportioned or granted to third persons, just like any other form of property. From the standpoint of an executory obligation which must be collected, the sense in which it interests us at this point, rent has many peculiarities.

The obligation can run only to the lessor, since rent is said to be incident to the reversion because it is basically an annual rendering of the profits of the land, and arises out of the reversion. Therefore the lessor cannot create a term with a rent payable to a third person, although after the rent is in existence as an incorporeal hereditament, he can grant it to the third person. Rent also must be a certain amount or capable of being reduced to certainty. At common law rents were divided into three classes, the distinguishing characteristic being the type of remedy available for collection of the rent.

A. Rent service was a rent to which some corporeal service (at the very least fealty) was incident. For nonpayment of such a rent the lord or lessor had an immediate and inherent right to use the common law device of self help called distress or distraint. In this procedure no judicial action was necessary; the lessor or his agent merely took possession of the personal property found on the premises, regardless of its ownership and held it for security for payment of the rent. The lessor could not sell the property but could merely hold it until he was paid.

B. Rent charge was a rent held by a person other than the original lessor or reversioner, where the right to use distress or distraint to enforce payment was provided for expressly by a clause in the lease.

C. Rent seck was a rent held by a person who did not have the right to use distress or distraint. In order to recover such a rent it would be necessary to use an action of covenant.

In the United States the classifications used at common law have been used in only a few of the older states. The reason for the classification no longer exists as every American state has some statutory form of procedure which takes the place of common law distress. Such a procedure is normally called by the old names of either distress or distraint, but it is probable that the common law form exists in only a few states. Rent with us is simply a matter of contract, where there are several remedies available. With the broadening of assumpsit the importance of distress has vanished.

B. EXPECTANT ESTATES, OR PRESENT ESTATES OF FUTURE ENJOYMENT

I. Interests Arising Prior to the Statute of Uses

Sec. 148. Nature of Expectant Estates. The estate concept imparted a "thinglikeness," or corporeal quality, to the estate in land as distinct from the land itself. Consequently, and this is one of the distinguishing characteristics of the Anglo-American law of real property, the estate could be subdivided into successive interests, the sum total of all the interests thus created being the estate itself. So far we have been concerned exclusively with interests of present enjoyment, and have discovered that such interests are distinguishable by quantum. The interests which we are about to examine have in themselves no reference to quantum. They are distinguished as to time of enjoyment. Their quantum is determined in just the same way as that of estates of present enjoyment. Consequently, any type of future or expectant estate can have any conceivable quantum.

a. *Right of Re-entry for Condition Broken (Power of Termination)*

Sec. 149. Right of Re-entry for Condition Broken (Power of Termination)—at Common Law. When a grantor created an estate in fee simple subject to a condition subsequent, he and his heirs retained the power of terminating that estate upon non-compliance with the condition. This power remaining in the grantor was not an estate, but merely the possibility, upon non-compliance with the condition, of acquiring an estate by exercising the option. For instance, where the grant was to A and his heirs, but if the property is ever used as a place of public amusement, the grantor and his heirs may re-enter, if the property was thereafter used by A or his heirs as a place of public amusement, the grantor and his heirs had the option of exercising their right of re-entry and thus terminating the estate of A or his heirs. This right of re-entry, of course, applied equally in all situations where an estate of any quantum was granted subject to a condition subsequent.

Sec. 150. Right of Re-entry for Condition Broken (Power of Termination)—Creation in Favor of Third Person at Common Law. The common law requirement of seisin necessitating a transfer of the seisin by the grantor at the time of the conveyance to the person who was to take or to an agent in his behalf made it impossible to create a right of re-entry in a person other than the grantor and his heirs. It could not be done by the transfer of seisin to such a person himself, because the seisin was being transferred to the taker of the estate subject to the condition, and that taker of the estate subject to the condition could not be considered as accepting the seisin on behalf of such other third person because their interests would be, in their very nature, antagonistic. Throughout the common law, it was impossible to create a right of re-entry, or to use more modern terminology, a power of termination, in a third person.

Sec. 151. Right of Re-entry for Condition Broken (Power of Termination)—Transfer to Third Person at Common Law. Since the right of re-entry so closely resembled a mere chose in action, and due to the policy against maintenance, choses in action were non-transferable at common law, the right of re-entry could not be transferred to a third person after it had been created. The very existence of the right also tended to lessen the free alienability of the land to which it attached. The courts, here as in all other situations, eager to destroy anything resembling a restraint on the power to alienate a complete estate, decided that an attempt to alienate the right of re-entry was not only abortive but also absolutely destructive of the right of re-entry, leaving a complete estate in the hands of the holder.

It should be noted that a statute in the reign of Henry VIII changed the position of the common law, with reference to the transferability of the right of re-entry on a term for life or for years. Under this statute, the right of re-entry was freely transferable so long as it was transferred along with the entire interest of the grantor.

The disability to create a power of termination in a third person caused no hardship after the enactment of the Statute of Uses and the Statute of Wills during the reign of Henry VIII. Under those statutes, the grantor could effectuate his object by means of executory limitations, which were freely transferable. Such executory limitations will be considered later in this work.

Sec. 152. Right of Re-entry for Condition Broken (Power of Termination)—in the United States. In the United States, rights of re-entry or powers of termination have been extremely common, from the earliest period. Recently with the development of mineral resources and the growth of the practice of conveying such mineral resources by means of determinable estates they have become even more common.

Sec. 153. Right of Re-entry for Condition Broken (Power of Termination)—Creation in Third Person in the United States. In this country, the cases have unhesitatingly followed the common law in the position that a right of re-entry cannot be created in favor of a third person. Like so many of the rules regarding expectant estates in the United States, this is an anachronistic survival of a rule based on a seisin concept in jurisdictions where the economic reasons for the existence of the seisin concept have never operated. Despite the failure of the reasons for the rule, however, the rule itself is too firmly entrenched to admit of question.

Sec. 154. Right of Re-entry for Condition Broken (Power of Termination)—Transfer to Third Person in the United States.[23] So far as the transferability of the power of termination to a third person is concerned, apparently the majority of our jurisdictions are in accord with the common law position and do not permit a transfer of the power of termination. There are several jurisdictions which expressly by statute permit such transfer and there are a few jurisdictions which by decisions permit the transfer after breach of the condition, but not prior thereto.

The Statute of Henry VIII is in force in most of our jurisdictions while in others there are local statutes having the same effect. In fact in no jurisdiction has the right of a transferee of the entire interest of the grantor to enforce the power of termination been denied.

With reference to the effect of an attempted transfer in those jurisdictions which follow the common law rule as to non-transferability, there are very few decisions, but all of those decisions are in accord with the common law that an

---

[23] American Law Institute, Restatement of Property. Tentative Draft Number 4, pp. 112-116. Proposed Final Draft, pp. 328, 329, 343.

attempted transfer is not only abortive but destructive of the power of termination.

The Statute of Uses or a statute reaching the same result is in force in the majority of the states, while the Statute of Wills is in force in all of the jurisdictions. Consequently, executory limitations are available to effectuate the purpose of the grantor. This undoubtedly accounts for the paucity of case material on disability to create a power of termination in a person other than the grantor or his heirs and on the transfer of such an interest.

Sec. 155. Right of Re-entry for Condition Broken (Power of Termination)—Devolution on Death at Common Law. The concept of seisin had a very great influence on the common law principles governing the matter of intestate succession. Where the creator of a right of re-entry died, descent was said to have been "cast" upon his heir. If that heir died before the occurrence of the condition, the right of re-entry descended not to his heir, but to the person who would have been the heir of the creator of the right of re-entry, had his death taken place at that time. The older law stated this position by saying that only the person last seised could constitute a "stock of descent," and since in that situation only the creator of the right had been seised, all descents had to be traced from him. This type of descent was called indiscriminately "descent" or "taking by representation."

Since at the common law, rights of re-entry could not be created in a third person and could not be transferred to a third person, their disposition after death could not be controlled by will.

Sec. 156. Right of Re-entry for Condition Broken (Power of Termination)—Devolution on Death in the United States.[24] In the United States, there have been occasional instances of the application of the common law principles of intestate succession, but in this country the general feeling is that powers of termination should descend in the same way

---

[24] American Law Institute, Restatement of Property. Tentative Draft Number 4, pp. 134-138.

as any other present interest of the same quantum under our modern intestate statutes.

Clearly enough, in the states in which such interests are transferable, they are also devisable. In addition, many jurisdictions by statute make any interest devisable which is descendible and in those jurisdictions we may have the anomalous situation that although the power of termination cannot be created in a third person or conveyed to a third person, it can be devised to him. Thus in the United States at the present, there is far greater control and power of transfer of the power of termination by will than there is by transaction *inter vivos*.

b. *Possibility of Reverter*

Sec. 157. Possibility of Reverter at Common Law and in the United States. When a grantor created an estate in fee simple subject to a special limitation he and his heirs retained a possibility that the estate might return to them on the contingency named or indicated. This interest remaining in the grantor was not an estate but merely a possibility of acquiring an estate on the happening of the contingency. It was known as a possibility of reverter. For instance, in a grant to A and his heirs so long as the property was used for conducting religious services, in the event that the property at some time was no longer used for the holding of religious services, the estate of A and his heirs automatically came to an end, and the estate in fee simple was said to "revert" or go back to the grantor and his heirs. This applied equally of course in all situations where an estate of any quantum had been granted subject to a special limitation.

Sec. 158. Possibility of Reverter—Creation in or Transfer to Third Person at Common Law. The same consideration which made the creation of a right of re-entry in a third person impossible and the transfer of that right to a third person impossible operated equally in the case of a possibility of reverter so that this interest also could not be created in or transferred to a third person.

With reference to the attempt to transfer such an interest to a third person, however, the consequence was quite different than that which resulted from an attempt to transfer to a third person a right of re-entry. Unlike the power of termination, which was simply an option requiring affirmative action on the part of the holder to terminate the estate, the possibility of reverter operated automatically. It had no resemblance therefore to a chose in action and there could be no fear of its transfer leading to maintenance. Consequently, an attempt to transfer a possibility of reverter, although abortive, did not extinguish the possibility of reverter.

After the passage of the Statute of Uses and the Statute of Wills, it became possible to create in a third person an interest very similar to the possibility of reverter. This interest was known as an executory limitation and was considered freely transferable. It will be treated in detail later in this work.

Sec. 159. Possibility of Reverter—Creation in or Transfer to Third Person in the United States. In the United States, decisions and statutes in many jurisdictions permit the transfer of the possibility of reverter to a third person, although it is still considered impossible to create such an interest in favor of a third person. Executory limitations have always been available to effectuate the purpose of the grantor in this country.

Sec. 160. Possibility of Reverter—Devolution on Death at Common Law. The rules as to devolution on the death intestate of the holder of a possibility of reverter were the same at common law as those with reference to the similar situation concerning the right of re-entry.

Sec. 161. Possibility of Reverter—Devolution on Death in the United States.[25] Only one jurisdiction has a statute expressly making the possibility of reverter devisable. In

---

[25] American Law Institute, Restatement of Property. Tentative Draft Number 4, pp. 52-53.

those jurisdictions with statutes providing that any interest which is descendible is devisable the point has arisen in only one jurisdiction and there the possibility of reverter was held to be non-devisable. Similarly in the largest group of jurisdictions where the terms of the statute are very broad, a few jurisdictions have held such interests non-devisable, while others have held the interests were covered by the statute and therefore devisable.

In brief, the situation as to devolution in the United States is not covered very extensively by case material, and such cases as do exist seem to be in hopeless conflict. Undoubtedly the possibility of construing such interests as executory limitations which are freely transferable, devisable and descendible, accounts for the paucity of decisions on these points, although it does not by any means explain the conflict in the cases which have arisen.

c. Reversions

Sec. 162. Reversions at Common Law and in the United States. When the holder of any estate of present enjoyment created in another person an estate whose duration was less than the durability of his own estate, obviously he had not granted his entire interest. The interest which the grantor retained in such a case was an estate of future enjoyment with the same quantum as that of his original estate. This interest retained by the grantor was called a "reversion." The name arose from the Latin verb *"reverti"* which was used in the earlier conveyances to indicate that after the estate granted had come to an end, the land would "revert" or return to the grantor. The estate granted was spoken of as the "particular" estate, from the Latin word *"particula,"* meaning portion. For example, A, the holder of a life estate, granted to B for life or for a term of years. By operation of law, according to the classical phrase, or in other words, simply because he had not granted all that he had, A had a reversion, the quantum of which was a life estate. The result as a practical matter was that if B predeceased A, or if the term for years expired before A died, A immediately had the right to possession and could hold possession until his death. Of course, had A predeceased B, or had he died before the termination of the term for years, B's estate would have come to an end at A's death, because as was pointed out when dealing with the subject of life estates, the life tenant could grant no more than he had, and, in that event, the existence of the reversion in A would have been rendered completely unimportant. In all of the above situations, the estate of B would have been called the particular estate.

It will be recalled that escheat was one incident of a grant of real property which was not abolished by the statute of Charles II in 1660. Thus escheat continued as an incident in English law long after the American colonies had adopted the common law. There has been some confusion in the use of the terms escheat and reversion, since on the face of it, they seem practically identical. In both, at the termination of the estate granted, the land returned to the grantor. Both were dependent on tenure, so that in a system of real property law which was actually alodial, neither concept could exist.

There was one very important distinction, however. Escheat operated only on an estate in fee simple, after all the heirs of the grantee had died out. A reversion, on the other hand, arose only on the grant of an interest less than that held by the grantor. The interest held by the grantor could at the highest be only an estate in fee simple, so that there was no reversion unless the particular estate granted by him had been less than an estate in fee simple.

Sec. 163. Reversions at Common Law and in the United States—Position of the Reversioner. Since the holder of a reversion was not in possession of the property, but had simply an interest which would eventually entitle him to possession, his rights, privileges, powers and immunities were considerably less than those of the holder of any present interest. He had, for example, no privilege of possession or present enjoyment, and consequently no rights against third persons who interfered with the enjoyment. He had the power of alienation and certain very important rights of action against the holder of the particular estate should the latter act in such a way as to impair the property to which the reversioner would ultimately succeed. These last, in themselves, were, of course, privileges, and important privileges, but they vary very widely from the privileges of the holder of an estate of present enjoyment.

Sec. 164. Reversions—Conveyances at Common Law. Since the word "reversion" had no connotation of quantum, and since the type of conveyance used was regulated by the quantum of the interest conveyed, there can be no simple all-inclusive statement of the methods of conveyance used to transfer a reversion or to create new interests in the reversion which would intervene between the particular estate and an ultimate reversion.

Since the typical reversion was in freehold, and in fact reversions of less than freehold were comparatively rare, we shall confine our attention to the difficulties attendant on the alienation of a reversion of freehold or upon the creation of new lesser estates of future enjoyment.

Due to the fact that the reversioner was not in possession of the land, the basic common law mode of conveying, that is, feoffment with livery of seisin, was not available to him, and his entry upon the land in order to make a conveyance by feoffment with livery of seisin would have constituted an actionable trespass against the holder of the particular estate in possession. It is from this fact that difficulties arose. Conveyancing around these difficulties developed as follows:

A. When the reversioner wished to convey his interest to the tenant in possession of the land, that is, to the holder of the particular estate, he could do so by means of a deed of release.

B. When the reversioner wished to convey his interest to a third person, at early law, we must distinguish between the case where the occupier of the land was a tenant holding by villein tenure, where he was a tenant for years, and where he was a freeholder.

1. As was pointed out in the chapter dealing with Tenures, the common law disregarded the customary rights of the tenant holding in villeinage. In the eyes of the law courts, such a tenant was simply occupying the land in the name of the reversioner, which meant that it was possible to convey the reversioner's interest by means of a feoffment accompanied by livery of seisin. It was usual to include in the transaction a recognition by the tenant of the transfer of the reversion. Obviously, with the disappearance of villein tenure, the possibility of conveying the reversioner's interest in this fashion also disappeared.

2. Where the tenant occupying the land was a tenant for years, at early law, the transfer of the reversion to a third person might be accomplished either by deed of grant, followed by attornment on the part of the tenant for years, or by feoffment with livery of seisin, since the tenant for years had no remedy against such a trespass. Attornment was simply the recognition by the tenant of the transfer of the lordship. In the period following that of Bracton, remedies having by that time been made available to the termor, it became impossible for the lord to proceed by way of feoffment with livery of seisin, unless he had first either obtained the consent of the termor, or had waited to enter upon the land until such time as the tenant, and his entire family were absent from the land.

3. Where the tenant was a freeholder, the reversioner had no right to enter upon the land and there make a feoffment with livery of seisin. Under these circumstances, a deed of grant was resorted to as the method of transferring the reversioner's interest. The tenant who was occupying the land had to attorn himself to the new lord, often making a nominal payment to him, in recognition of his right of lordship. The conveyance was not effectual until the tenant had attorned, but attornment could be compelled.

C. In all of the above situations, the fine was available and useful as a method of conveying the reversion. The advantage of the fine in this connection was that if a fine were levied, there was a regular procedure for compelling the tenant occupying the land to appear before the court and confess the terms of his tenure. Unless there was good reason for the tenant's refusal to attorn, he would then either be compelled to attorn himself or be attorned by the court.

The necessity for attornment was abolished by a statute in 1705, during the reign of Anne.

Sec. 165. Reversions—Conveyances in the United States. In the United States, since feoffment with livery of seisin was already archaic and other methods of conveyancing were in vogue at the time of the settlement of the colonies, many of the problems which had disturbed lawyers for three centuries in England did not arise. Since our conveyances do not require going upon the land, any conveyance available for the transfer of present interests in fee simple has always been available for the transfer of a reversion, regardless of whether or not the transferee was the holder of the particular estate or a third person. The requirement as to attornment has been abolished in many states by statutes patterned on the statute of Anne, and in no state is there convincing evidence that an attornment ever was necessary.

Sec. 166. Reversions—Devolution on Death at Common Law. As has already been mentioned, the concept of seisin greatly influenced the common law principles governing the matter of intestate succession. When the holder of a reversion died intestate, descent was "cast" upon his heir. Thereafter that heir had the power of transferring his interest of future enjoyment either by conveyance *inter vivos* or by will. If, however, he died intestate before the interest had become one of present enjoyment, and without having exercised his power of conveyance *inter vivos*, he could not be a new "stock of descent." In order for one claiming to be allowed to take in that event, it was necessary for him to show that he was the heir of the person last seised of the land. This succession to the interest after death was known as a "descent" or "taking by representation."

After the passage of the Statute of Wills, the holder of a reversion could devise it on his death, and since his heir took by purchase in that event, he could constitute a new stock of descent, and himself had the power to devise his interest of future enjoyment should he die before it had become a possessory estate.

Sec. 167. Reversions—Devolution on Death in the United States.[26] In the United States, statutes in practically every jurisdiction have abolished the common law principles relating to intestate succession. In case of the death intestate of the holder of an interest of future enjoyment, the person who takes by intestate succession is ascertained finally and unchangeably by the facts as they exist at the death of the holder of the interest. That person is a new stock of descent as to the reversion. It is no longer necessary that the person claiming as heir in order to be entitled by intestate succession be the heir of the person last seised of the land.

In this country, from the very beginning, any reversion could be devised by the holder thereof.

d. Remainders

Sec. 168. Remainders at Common Law. Where the holder of an estate in land granted away a particular estate followed by estates the sum total of which might or might not exhaust the grantor's entire estate, the verb used in conveying all of the interests subsequent to the particular estate was the Latin verb *"remanere"*—the land was to remain out. From this verb such interests were called remainders and the persons who took such interests were called remaindermen. Unlike the reversion which arose merely by operation of law, because the grantor had not conveyed his entire interest, the remainder was created expressly by the grantor. Obviously,

---

[26] American Law Institute, Restatement of Property. **Tentative Draft Number 4, pp. 52-53.**

if the holder of a fee simple created successive estates, one of which was an estate in fee simple, no interest limited to take effect subsequent to that could be valid, since the grantor had already given away all that he had. This is usually expressed by the cliché that no remainder could be granted after a fee simple.

Sec. 169. Remainders—Effect of Common Law Concept of Seisin in the Creation of Remainders. One difficulty in the creation of a remainder and a problem which vexed the older real property lawyers was the manner in which the remainderman acquired seisin. Finally, the courts decided that the holder of the particular estate accepted the seisin not only for himself but also on behalf of the remainderman. As a consequence of this, several rules arose which dominated the law of remainders throughout the common law period.

Sec. 170. Remainders—Common Law Rule Requiring that the Particular Estate and the Remainder be Created in the Same Conveyance. Since the holder of the particular estate was taking seisin for the remainderman, it naturally followed that the remainder or remainders must be created at the same moment as the particular estate, by means of the same conveyance, due to the fact that seisin passed only by that conveyance. For instance, X, the holder of an estate in fee simple makes the following grants in a single conveyance, "To A for life, remainder to B in fee simple." A, the holder of the particular estate, receives seisin due to the conveyance, and accepts that seisin not only for himself but also for the remainderman, B. Had the grantor made use of two separate conveyances, one in order to grant the life estate to A, and the other to grant the estate in fee simple to B, A could not have been said to have taken seisin for B, since the seisin passed from X to A at the moment of the first conveyance, at a time when B had no interest. B's remainder in that case would fail due to the fact that there was no way in which B could acquire seisin.

Sec. 171. Remainders—Common Law Rule Requiring that Particular Estate be Estate of Freehold. The second common law rule governing the creation of a remainder was that the particular estate that preceded the remainder must itself be an estate of freehold. This rule arose because it was only a freeholder who received seisin. The freehold estates, it will be recalled, were estates in fee simple, in fee tail, and life estates. Obviously then the precedent estate must have been one in fee tail or for life, since had the grantor granted an estate in fee simple, he would have exhausted his entire interest, and there would be nothing that he could give to anyone. Where X, the holder of an estate in fee simple, granted Blackacre to A for life, remainder to B in fee simple, A was given a freehold estate and so received seisin, which he held for B as well as for himself. Had the grant been to A for twenty years, remainder to B, A would not have been given a freehold estate, would consequently not have received seisin, and so B's interest would have failed, since in that event, it was not possible for A to hold seisin for B.

There was one exception to the rule that the particular estate must be one of freehold, however. If the grantor were creating an estate of less than freehold to be followed immediately by an estate of freehold held by a person now ascertained and now in being, he could make the conveyance to the holder of the freehold estate, who would then deliver the possession to the taker of the estate of less than freehold. For instance, in the above case, where X wished to create a nonfreehold interest, a term for years in A, to be followed immediately by a freehold estate in fee simple in B, a living person, he could effectuate his purpose by conveying the estate in fee simple to B by feoffment with livery of seisin, and B would then deliver possession to A. The interest that B received, under those circumstances, however, was not conceived of as being a remainder, but was spoken of as an estate subject to a term.

Sec. 172. Remainders—Common Law Rule Requiring that the Remainder be Limited to Take Effect Immediately upon the Termination of the Precedent Estate. The next common law rule regulating the creation of remainders was that an estate could not be created which would take effect in remainder otherwise than immediately upon the termination of the next precedent estate. In other words, there could be no gap in the seisin, since there would then be no way in which the seisin could arise in the holder of such an interest. For instance, where X, the holder of an estate in fee simple, granted Blackacre to A for life, remainder to B six months after the death of A, the remainder to B would fail, since there would be a gap in the seisin. During the six months between the death of A and the time when C's interest was to commence, the seisin would be nowhere, that is to say, it would be "in abeyance," which was impossible, according to the common law ideas.

Sec. 173. Remainders—Common Law Rule Providing that the Remainder Could Not be Limited to Take Effect in Derogation of the Precedent Estate. Another rule governing the creation of remainders at common law, flowing directly from the concept of seisin, was that no remainder could be created which was limited to come into effect by cutting off the prior estate, because such a limitation would make the interest of the holder of the particular estate antagonistic to the interest of the remainderman. Under such circumstances, the holder of the particular estate could not be regarded as accepting seisin on behalf of the holder of the remainder. For instance, where X, the holder of an estate in fee simple, granted Blackacre to A for life, remainder to B, the remainder to B was good, since B's interest was limited to take effect upon the regular ending of A's interest, and not to take effect by way of cutting off A's interest before its regular ending. However, had the terms of the grant been "to A for life, but upon B's marriage to C, remainder to C," the remainder to C would have failed, since in that event C's interest was to take effect in derogation of A's, and A could not therefore be conceived as holding seisin for C, whose interest was antagonistic to his own. Moreover, in effect, the grantor had provided that there should be a power of termination of A's interest in C, in the event of B's marriage to C, and as was pointed out in the sections dealing with powers of termination, such an interest could not be created in favor of a third person, such as C.

Sec. 174. Remainders—Distinction Between Vested and Contingent Remainders. Originally the only remainders recognized by the law were those created in favor of an ascertained person, and which were bound to take effect merely upon the termination of the preceding estate. Even in the early law, however, a need was felt for another type of remainder—one which would permit the grantor to control the disposition of his property not only to his contemporaries but to persons as yet unborn and which would permit him to control the disposition of his property in accordance with the happening of future events. In 1430 the first remainder of this new type was recognized. It was called a contingent remainder. The other type of remainder which had been recognized previously was from that time on spoken of as a vested remainder. A vested remainder is usually defined as a remainder which has the present capacity of taking effect merely on the termination of the preceding estates. In other words, in a vested remainder nothing interferes with the enjoyment of the remainderman except the fact that the estate is in the possession of a prior holder; immediately upon the termination of that prior interest, he is ready to come into the enjoyment of a present estate.

Sec. 175. Vested Remainders—Position of the Remainderman. The holder of a vested remainder was in a position with reference to the land very similar to that enjoyed by the holder of a reversion. He did not have the possession of the land, and did not therefore have possessory remedies against those who infringed upon the enjoyment of the present possessor, but he did have the privilege of receiving the land at the expiration of the particular estate in substantially the same condition in which the holder of the present estate had received it, subject to normal wear and tear. He also had a remedy by writ of waste to protect this privilege. In addition, if a third person damaged the land in such a way that the damage was permanent, spoken of as a damage to the freehold, the holder of the remainder had the right to recover from the third person compensation for the damage to his interest.

Sec. 176. Vested Remainders in the United States. In the United States, vested remainders have always been recognized and have been treated just as they were at common law.

Sec. 177. Vested Remainders—Conveyances at Common Law. Vested remainders, since they were comparatively certain interests, could be alienated just as could any other certain interest in land. The type of conveyance applicable was determined to a large extent by the quantum of the interest. Thus a remainder which was a non-freehold interest was alienable, but the conveyances applicable were those available to any transfer of a non-freehold interest. In conveying remainders of freehold, feoffment with livery of seisin was of course not available to the remainderman, since he himself had no seisin. The type of conveyance, then, depended on the position of the grantee with reference to the land.

A. If the remainder were to be granted to the holder of the particular estate, the holder of another remainder, or the holder of an ultimate reversion, the type of conveyance used was the deed of release.

B. If the remainder were being granted to a third person, the method of conveyance was the deed of grant.

Sec. 178. Vested Remainders—Conveyances in the United States. In the United States, similarly, releases and deeds of grant, depending on the position of the grantee, were used from the earliest times to convey remainders. They have been almost entirely supplanted, however, by conveyances under modern statutes which reach a similar result.

Sec. 179. Vested Remainders—Devolution on Death at the Common Law and in the United States. At the early common law, on the death intestate of the holder of a vested remainder, the rules of descent with reference to the person last seised operated, and descent was "cast" on the heir. The situation then was the same as with reference to reversions.

The changes noted in the United States with reference to reversions apply equally to vested remainders.

With reference to vested remainders, the law controlling devolution on death went through the same mutations both in England and in this country as it did with reference to reversions.

Sec. 180. Contingent Remainders at Common Law. We have already pointed out that in 1430 the courts first recognized an interest created in a person, not yet in being, which was spoken of as a contingent remainder. This first contingent remainder recognized was one in favor of the heirs of a living person. For a considerable time, any attempt at greater originality on the part of grantors was sternly repressed. Finally, in the middle of the sixteenth century, the courts recognized the validity of remainders dependent on contingencies other than the death of a living person.

A contingent remainder was a remainder which came into effect only on the happening of some condition in addition to the termination of the preceding particular estate, which condition might conceivably happen before or after the termination of the preceding estate. For example, where A, the holder of an estate in fee simple in Blackacre, granted Blackacre to A until C marry B, and then over to D, D's interest was a contingent remainder. In addition to the termination of the preceding estate of A, the condition that B and C marry must happen before D's interest could take effect. Obviously, B and C might never marry each other, or they might do so only after A's interest had been terminated by his death, or after D, himself, had died. In any one of those situations, D's interest would never take effect by becoming an estate of present enjoyment.

Sec. 181. Contingent Remainders—Fearne's Classification. In his monumental treatise on Contingent Remainders, Charles Fearne classified [27] them, merely for purposes of convenience, as follows:

---

[27] Fearne, Charles, An Essay on the Learning of Contingent Remainders and Executory Devises (3d Am. ed. 1853), pp. 3-7.

"*First,* Where the determination of the preceding estate itself depends on an event which may never happen; as if A. makes a feoffment to the use of B. till C. return from Rome, and after such return of C. then to remain over in fee; here the particular estate is limited to determine on the return of C. an event which possibly may never happen; and therefore the remainder, which depends on such contingent determination of the preceding estate is dubious and contingent. So where a fine was levied to the use of A. and the heirs male of his body, until he the said A. should do such a thing; and after such a thing done by the said A. to the use of B. in tail; A. died without issue, and without performing the condition; and it was adjudged that the remainder was contingent and never took place.

"*Secondly,* where some uncertain event, unconnected with, and collateral to the determination of the preceding estate, is, by the nature of the limitation, to precede the remainder; as if a lease be made to A. for life, remainder to B. for life, and if B. die before A. remainder to C. for life, here the event of B.'s dying before A. does not in the least affect the determination of the particular estate, nevertheless it must precede and give effect to C.'s remainder; but such event is dubious, it may or may not happen, and the remainder depending on it is therefore contingent. So if lands be given to A. in tail, and if B. come to Westminster-hall such a day, to B. in fee; here B.'s coming to Westminster-hall has no connection with the determination of A.'s estate; but as it is an uncertain event, and the remainder to B. is not to take place unless it should happen, such remainder is therefore a contingent remainder.

"*Thirdly,* Where a remainder is limited to take effect upon an event, which, although it certainly must happen some time or other yet may not happen till after the determination of the particular estate;—as if a lease be made to J.S. for life, and after the death of J.D. the lands to remain to another in fee; now it is certain that J.D. must die some time or other, but his death may not happen till after the determination of the particular estate by the death of J.S. and therefore such remainder is contingent.—So in case of a lease for life to A. and after the death of A. and M., the remainder to B. in fee, this is a contingent remainder; for the particular estate being only for the life of A. and the remainder not commence till after the death of A. and M., if A. die before M., the particular estate will end before the remainder can commence; which is very possible, and therefore such remainder is contingent. So if a feoffment be to the use of A. for 21 years if he shall so long live, and after his death to the use of B. in fee; here A. may survive the 21 years; if he should, the particular estate would determine before the remainder could commence, and therefore such remainder is contingent; and, being so, is void, for want of a preceding freehold to support it, as will appear hereafter.

"*Fourthly,* Where a remainder is limited to a person not ascertained, or not in being at the time when such limitation is made;—as if a lease be made to one for life, remainder to the right heirs of J.S. now there can be no such person as the right heir of J.S. until after the death of J.S. (for *nemo est haeres viventis*) which may not happen till after the determination of the particular estate by the death of tenant for life, therefore such remainder is contingent.—So where a remainder is limited to the first son of B. who has no son then born; here B. may never have a son, or if he should, the particular estate may determine before the birth of such son, therefore this remainder is contingent.—So if an estate be limited to two for life, remainder to the *survivor* of them in fee, the remainder is contingent, for it is uncertain who will be the survivor."

Sec. 182. Contingent Remainders—Rules Governing Creation of Contingent Remainders at Common Law—Rule Requiring that the Particular Estate and the Remainder be

Created in the Same Conveyance—Rule Requiring that the Particular Estate be an Estate of Freehold. The four basic principles arising from the concept of seisin stated in the foregoing sections applied equally, and for the same reasons, to contingent remainders, and with reference to contingent remainders, some of them had consequences which did not follow in the case of vested remainders.

A.   The remainder and the particular estate must be created in one conveyance.

B.   The particular estate must be an estate of freehold. Since this rule flows directly from the concept of seisin which required seisin to be in someone at all times, if the contingency upon which the remainder was to be determined did not occur before the termination of the particular estate, the contingent remainder failed. For example, in a grant to A for life, remainder to the first-born son of B, if A died before B had a son, the contingent remainder in favor of that unborn son of B failed, since in that case there was no one to hold the seisin, which was therefore placed in abeyance. The courts were all the more ready to reach this result, since it prevented the creation of any interest tending to restrain the alienation of land. This led directly to the devices of alternate contingent remainders or, as they are sometimes called, contingent remainders with a double aspect. For example, a grant to A for life, and on his death to his surviving children, and if he have no surviving children, then over to B. The value of such a grant lies in the fact that one of the remainders is bound to take effect.

Sec. 183.   Contingent Remainders—Destructibility at Common Law. In discussing life estates, it was said that where the life tenant purported to grant more than he had by a feoffment with livery of seisin or a fine or a common recovery he forfeited his life estate. If there were any contingent remainders dependent on that life estate, its forfeiture would destroy the estate of freehold and necessarily the seisin. In this case also the contingent remainder was destroyed. The same result followed so far as contingent remainders were concerned if the holder of the life estate forfeited his life estate by reason of some criminal activity, such as treason.

Sec. 184. Contingent Remainders—Development of Device of Trustees to Preserve Contingent Remainders. To avoid the result of failure of the contingent remainder due to forfeiture of the freehold estate, two prominent conveyancers, Sir Orlando Bridgman and Sir Geoffrey Palmer, during the period of the Commonwealth, in the middle of the seventeenth century, at a time when forfeitures for treason were only too common, invented the device of trustees to preserve contingent remainders. In this device, after the particular estate an estate was inserted to trustees, the quantum of which was for the duration of the particular estate, and immediately following this came the contingent remainder. For example, to A for life, then to B, C, and D for the life of A as trustees to preserve contingent remainders, then to the heirs of X. Here in the event that A forfeited his life estate either by treason or by a tortious feoffment, the estate of the trustees, the next vested estate of freehold, came into possession, retained the seisin and thus saved the contingent remainder.

Sec. 185. Contingent Remainders—Doctrine of Merger at Common Law—Failure of Contingent Remainder. Another consequence of this requirement of a preceding estate of freehold to support a contingent remainder arose from the common law concept of merger. Because of the estate concept, it was possible to carve several lesser estates out of a greater one. If then one of those lesser estates came into the hands of one who held a greater estate in the same land, the lesser estate was said to be destroyed and merged in the greater. For example, A, the holder of an estate in fee simple, grants to B for life, remainder to the heirs of C. A has not granted his entire interest, since on the termination of B's life estate, there may be no heirs of C. A retains a reversion. If A and B should both convey their interest to X, the reversion and the life estate would then be held by one person. They would merge, and the life-estate, the lesser estate, would be destroyed. Immediately, then, the contingent remainder in the heirs of C would also be destroyed because there would no longer be a precedent estate of freehold to support it—there would be no one holding seisin for the contingent remainder-man.

It should be noted, however, as an exception to this rule, that merger would not occur where the greater and lesser estate united in the hands of the holder simultaneously with the creation of the contingent remainder. An extremely common example is the following: T dies, leaving a will in which he devises land to A for life, remainder to the heirs of X. If A were also the residuary devisee of T or the heir of T, he would simultaneously acquire the life estate and the reversion. There would be no merger, however, because the courts felt that to create a merger in this situation would be to nullify the will. A deed creating the same interests would be construed in the same way.

Sec. 186. Rule in Shelley's Case. It is probably appropriate at this point in the discussion of merger to mention briefly a very famous rule of law, the so-called Rule in Shelley's Case. This rule was actually established in the Provost of Beverley's Case in the fourteenth century. It was reaffirmed however in Shelley's Case, towards the end of the reign of Elizabeth, in 1581. The case was extremely well argued by very eminent counsel, and since that time the rule then reaffirmed has been spoken of as the Rule in Shelley's Case. It operated in this situation. Where a life estate was granted to A and a remainder to his heirs, which remainder would normally have been construed as a contingent remainder, due to an involved argument as to the actual intent of the grantor, occasioned by the complicated rules of descent in which great stress was placed on the stock of descent, the courts in order to effectuate what they apprehended to be the intent of the grantor, disregarded the contingent remainder, or, as they stated it, executed the remainder in the ancestor, giving him a fee simple, instead of a life estate. The customary statement of the Rule is: Where a life estate is given to an ancestor followed either mediately or immediately by a remainder to his heirs, the words "to his heirs" are construed as words of limitation and not as words of purchase.

Sec. 187. Contingent Remainders—Remainder in Favor of Child En Ventre Sa Mère. The first limitation on the operation of the rule that caused a contingent remainder to fail when the event had not happened before the termination of the particular estate of freehold was the invention of the device of trustees to preserve contingent remainders. The second limitation on the operation of the rule was a decision by the House of Lords at the very end of the sixteenth century. A life estate was limited to A, followed by a contingent remainder to his first-born son. A died, his wife then being pregnant. Shortly thereafter she was delivered of a child. The common law courts held that the contingent remainder failed. The House of Lords completely disregarded the rigorous logic which had impelled the courts to their conclusion and decided that for the purpose of this rule a child *en ventre sa mère* was in being. A few years later this position was reaffirmed by statute.

Sec. 188. Contingent Remainders—Common Law Rule Requiring that the Remainder be Limited to Take Effect Immediately upon the Termination of the Precedent Estate—Common Law Rule Providing that the Remainder Could Not be Limited to Take Effect in Derogation of the Precedent Estate. So far as the creation of contingent remainders was concerned, it was true that just as in the creation of vested remainders, an estate could not be created to take effect in remainder otherwise than immediately upon the termination of the next preceding estate, and there could be no creation of a subsequent estate in remainder which was to take effect by cutting off a prior estate. After the enactment of the Statute of Uses and the Statute of Wills, during the reign of Henry VIII, it was possible to create executory limitations which were subject to conditions precedent and which would either foreshorten the preceding interest or arise after a gap. The courts, however, steadfastly continued to construe as a contingent remainder any interest which could possibly be so construed, thus subjecting the interest to all of the possibilities of destruction and failure stated above.

Sec. 189. Contingent Remainders—Position of the Contingent Remainderman at Common Law. In the fourth class of contingent remainder as classified by Fearne, there was of course no person holding the interest so that any discussion of the legal relationships of the holder of a contingent remainder must be strictly limited to holders of contingent remainders of the first three classes. The position of such a contingent remainderman was much weaker than that of the vested remainderman. He had no possession and consequently no possessory remedies. His interest was so slight and his ultimate enjoyment so problematical that at common law he was never granted any rights of action either against third persons or against holders of the precedent estates who altered the condition of the land. His only privilege was that of waiting patiently for the happening of the event. The happening of the event did not necessarily give him the right to possession, however. For example, if the land were granted to A for life, remainder to the heirs of B, if B died while A was still living, the heirs of B were thereby ascertained, but they would not be entitled to the land until the termination of A's estate. Their position was immensely improved, however, by the happening of the event. They were now vested remaindermen, with all the rights, privileges, powers and immunities of vested remaindermen.

Sec. 190. Contingent Remainders—Rules Governing Creation in the United States—Rule Requiring that the Particular Estate and the Remainder be Created in the Same Conveyance. Contingent remainders have always been recognized in the United States. In the beginning, they were treated in the same way as in England at common law, although the concept of seisin in most ways was never an appreciable force in American law, but in the law governing contingent remainders the concept and its consequences were rigorously applied.

From the very beginning of our history until the present day it has been required that the remainder and the particular estate be created in one conveyance. This rule still holds despite the fact that feoffment with livery of seisin as a method of conveying is unknown with us. The reason for the rule is non-existent, but the rule itself persists.

Sec. 191. Contingent Remainders—Rules Governing Creation in the United States—Rule Requiring that Particular Estate be an Estate of Freehold—Failure of Remainder. The particular estate preceding the contingent remainder must be an estate of freehold. Although we have never had feudal obligations and the necessity that the land be seised at all times is therefore purely an academic necessity, this rule has been constantly a part of our law. The first consequence of this rule in England that a remainder will fail if the event does not occur before the termination of the preceding estate has been changed in over half of the jurisdictions by statute and in a few more by decisions.[28] In the other jurisdictions apparently a contingent remainder can still fail in this manner. This is natural termination of the contingent remainder as opposed to destruction of the contingent remainder.

Sec. 192. Contingent Remainders—Destructibility in the United States.[29] The next consequence, destruction by tortious feoffment, fine or common recovery and merger, has been expressly changed by statute in half of the states and by express declaration in a few more. In only a few jurisdictions are there cases definitely recognizing the power to destroy a contingent remainder. It would seem then that the very definite trend in this country has been to negative the most important consequences of this particular rule.

Sec. 193. Contingent Remainders—Rules Governing Creation in the United States—Rule Requiring that the Remainder be Limited to Take Effect Immediately upon the

---

[28] Note (1925) 11 Cornell Law Quarterly, 408-416.
[29] Note (1925) 11 Cornell Law Quarterly, 408.

Termination of the Precedent Estate. The rule that an estate in remainder could not be created which would take effect otherwise than immediately on the termination of the next preceding estate applied equally to contingent remainders. In about three-quarters of the states, there has been no change in this position. In the other quarter, however, principally in western jurisdictions, statutes exist which permit the creation of remainders of this type.

Sec. 194. Contingent Remainders—Rules Governing Creation in the United States—Rule Providing that the Remainder Could Not be Limited to Take Effect in Derogation of the Precedent Estate. There has been no appreciable change in the United States so far as the rule that there could be no creation of a subsequent estate which was limited to come into effect by cutting off a prior estate is concerned. No change was necessary in this rule since after the enactment of the Statute of Uses and the Statute of Wills, interests of this type could be created, and since there was no possibility of construing such interests as contingent remainders, the consequence mentioned above was not nearly so effective in this case.

Sec. 195. Contingent Remainders—Position of Contingent Remainderman in the United States. With reference to the position of the contingent remainderman, in the many jurisdictions which have abolished the destructibility of contingent remainders, the reasons no longer apply for denying him some consideration with reference to damage to the land. In such jurisdictions, his position should be like that of the vested remainderman. In the present state of the case authority, however, the holder of a contingent remainder has no remedy at law for waste, although courts of equity will, on his complaint, enjoin future waste and in a few jurisdictions have been willing to compensate him for past waste. The reason usually given for the rule of law is "that it cannot be known in advance of the happening of the contingency whether he will suffer damage or loss by the waste; and if the estate never vested in him, he would be paid for that which he had not lost."[30]

Sec. 196. Contingent Remainders—Conveyances at Common Law. Since, originally, a contingent remainder was regarded as a possibility that an estate might arise at some future time, rather than as an estate in the land, it could not be alienated *inter vivos,* except by fine or common recovery. One consideration that impelled the common law judges to reach this conclusion was the feeling that permitting alienation of contingent remainders might encourage maintenance. Another reason was their feeling that allowing alienation would complicate titles.

At early common law, a contingent remainder might, however, be released to the owner of the estate in possession or in remainder. Later in the history of the common law, two methods developed by means of which contingent remainders could be transferred. When a grantor conveyed land to which he had no title, and in the conveyance warranted the title, if he subsequently acquired the title, he was said to be estopped to assert it as against his grantee. This doctrine was applied to transfers of contingent remainders so that in effect a contingent remainder could be transfered by means of estoppel. It was not perfect transferability due to the possibility that intervening rights might arise.

The courts of equity have always been accustomed to enforcing a contract for the sale of land by compelling the reluctant party to perform. There is also an equitable principle that equity considers done what should be done. When the holder of a contingent remainder purported to transfer that remainder so far as the courts of equity were concerned, the transfer was effective, and after the occurrence of the event, an equity court would compel the holder of the contingent remainder to execute a conveyance which would be recognized by courts of law. This also provided an effective

---

[30] Watson v. Wolff-Goldman Realty Co., 95 Ark. 18, 128 S.W. 581, Ann. Cas. 1912A 540 (1910).

means of transferring contingent remainders, which was not however complete transferability since there was still a possibility of intervening equities.

Obviously the above discussion applies only to remainders of the first three of Fearne's classes. In a remainder of the fourth class speaking of transferability or non-transferability is pointless since there is no person whose conduct can raise the question.

Sec. 197. Contingent Remainders—Conveyances in the United States.[31] In the United States, the above rules as to transferability that prevailed in England have been used very extensively. In addition, well over half of our jurisdictions have by statute expressly made contingent remainders transferable. Consequently, there is only a handful of American jurisdictions in which contingent remainders are non-transferable.

Sec. 198. Contingent Remainders—Devolution on Death at Common Law. In the early history of the common law, the rules applying to the intestate devolution of contingent remainders were the same as those applying to intestate devolution of reversions and vested remainders, and they have gone through the same mutations. Obviously, these rules could apply only to remainders in which the person is ascertained, that is, to remainders of Fearne's first three classes, and where the remainder is not so limited that it depends on the person's survival of the event.

In the sixteenth century, after the passage of the Statute of Uses and the Statute of Wills, the courts still refused to permit the power to control the devolution of contingent remainders by will. By a gradual process of decision, however, this power was recognized in the eighteenth century.

Sec. 199. Contingent Remainders—Devolution on Death in the United States. In the United States, contingent remainders have always been devisable so long as the remainder

---

[31] American Law Institute, Restatement of Property. Tentative Draft Number 4, pp. 122-134. Proposed Final Draft, pp. 332-337.

was in favor of an ascertained person (there is a slight exception in New York and in those few jurisdictions which have adopted the New York Code of Real Property), and where the remainder was not so limited that it depended on the named person's survival of the happening of the event.

II. New Interests Arising Under the Statute of Uses

a. Executory Interests

Sec. 200. Executory Interests—Rise of Executory Interests—Effect of the Statute of Uses. The evolution of uses prior to the Statute of Uses has already been considered in two connections, with reference to the methods of conveyancing and with reference to devisability. In addition to recognizing methods of conveyancing and permitting control of the devolution of property on death, the court of Chancery permitted grantors to avoid the effects of the rules of seisin by creating two types of interest which would have been impossible at common law. In discussing remainders, we noted that one consequence of the requirement that seisin go out of the grantor to the grantees at the moment of the conveyance was that it was impossible to create a remainder otherwise than a vested remainder of freehold which was not preceded by an estate of freehold on the termination of which the remainder would immediately take effect. For example, if A attempted to convey to B for ten years, and then to the heirs of C, the heirs of C took no interest. Or if A attempted to convey property to his wife for her life, and after her death the property to be accumulated until the youngest child reached the age of 21, and then to the surviving children, the interest to the children would be absolutely invalid. In both cases, there was a gap in the seisin which was fatal to all succeeding interests.

If, on the other hand, A conveyed in fee simple to X to the use of B for ten years, then to the heirs of C, so far as the common law courts were concerned, the legal title was held by X and all requirements of seisin were satisfied. The ecclesiastical courts and later the Chancellor had no hesitation in compelling X to honor the conditions of the gift. Similarly, if A conveyed to X to the use of his widow for life, and after her death the property to be accumulated until the youngest child attained the age of 21, and then to the surviving children, the courts of equity recognized the rights of the children.

Another consequence of the rule of seisin requiring that seisin go out of the grantor to the grantees at the time of the conveyance was that a second interest the effect of which was to cut off the enjoyment of the prior interest was invalid. Since the interests of the two holders were antagonistic, the first taker could not be said to accept seisin on behalf of the second. For example, if A conveyed to B for life, but if he marry C, then over to D for life, D received no interest according to the courts of common law. But if A conveyed to X to the use of B for life, but if he marry C, then over to D for life, the courts of common law were satisfied with X as a holder of the seisin and the Chancellor would enforce the uses and the object of the grantor would be effectuated. The passage of the Statute of Uses, whose terms are stated in section 65, affected all of these interests recognized by the Chancellor but not by the law courts, by making them legal interests. Thus, in the examples given above, after the passage of the Statute of Uses even the law courts recognized the beneficiaries of the uses as holders of the interests.

Sec. 201. Executory Interests—Effect of the Statute of Wills—Springing Executory Uses, Springing Executory Devises, Shifting Executory Uses, Shifting Executory Devises. A very liberal construction of the Statute of Wills, enacted in 1540, just four years after the Statute of Uses, enabled a testator to create the same interests without the sham of setting up use devisees who would only serve as conduits of title. These interests created under the Statute of Wills operated in exactly the same way as those under the Statute of Uses. The interests which arose either after a non-freehold estate or after a gap in time were called springing executory uses or springing executory devises, depending on whether they arose under the Statute of Uses or under the Statute of Wills. The interests which cut off the preceding interests were called shifting executory uses or shifting executory devises, depending on whether they arose under the Statute of Uses or under the Statute of Wills. Thus in the reign of Henry VIII, four new legal future interests developed. The common term for all four is executory interests or limitations, and since the holders of any one of these four types of interest had the same rights, privileges, powers, and immunities, regardless of the type of interest, from this point on, we shall treat them as a single interest in the land.

Sec. 202. **Executory Interests—Treatment of Executory Interests by the Courts of Common Law.** Since an executory interest followed the happening of an event which cut off the preceding interest or followed the happening of an event which terminated a gap in time, both of which closely resembled the conditions precedent with which the courts were familiar in handling contingent remainders, an attempt was made shortly after the recognition of executory interests to assimilate them to contingent remainders. From their recognition until the end of the sixteenth century, their status was somewhat dubious. The attempt was to assimilate the executory interest to contingent remainders so far as liability to natural termination and liability to destruction were concerned. This would have rendered the new interests comparatively innocuous. Various decisions in the latter part of the sixteenth century treated executory interests in the same way as contingent remainders. However, in the opening years of the seventeenth century, when the common law courts realized that if they subjected executory interests to the same hazards as contingent remainders, the courts of equity would not follow these results, and the equity courts had the favor of the Crown, the common law courts did an abrupt about-face and held not only that executory interests were valid, but that they were indestructible.

Sec. 203. Executory Interests—Position of the Holder of an Executory Interest at Common Law and in Equity. So far as the condition of the holder of an executory interest was concerned, his position was midway between that of the holder of a vested remainder and that of the holder of a contingent remainder. His interest was subject to a condition precedent to coming into possession like that of the contingent remainderman, but it was not subject to destruction which brought it somewhat closer to that of a vested remainderman. As against the holder of the particular estate he had no action of waste at common law. This action had crystallized long before his interest was recognized and in the crystallization he had no place. The courts of equity would however protect him against future waste by the holder of a life estate by injunction, and for past waste would assess damages and impound them subject to the happening of the contingency. So far as the holder of an executory interest was concerned, he apparently had no recovery for damages occasioned by the act of a third person.

Sec. 204. Executory Interests—Construction of Executory Limitation as a Contingent Remainder, Wherever Possible. The indestructibility of the executory interest raised anew an old problem which had long vexed the common law judges. From an early period in the common law every time that grantors had created an interest which looked as though it would make possible the control of the devolution of property over a long period, the courts had sanctioned some method of cutting off such an interest. This had not been necessary in the case of contingent remainders, due to their destructibility. The recognition of these new indestructible interests raised the problem afresh. This tendency on the part of the courts first evidenced itself in a rule that if an interest could conceivably take effect as a contingent remainder, it must be so construed, thus rendering it liable to destruction. This restricted the field of operation of executory limitations.

Sec. 205. Executory Interests—Rule Against Perpetuities. As to those limitations which could not possibly take effect by way of contingent remainder, there was still a possibility of the creation of a limitation which would endure for a long period and thus restrict the alienability of the land. To this undesirable limitation the courts applied the term "perpetuity." This was a new use for a word which had done duty in stigmatizing practically any interest tending towards inalienability. The rule needed to curb this deplorable tendency was first enunciated clearly in 1681, in the Duke of Norfolk's Case. According to the Rule against Perpetuities, as finally settled, any interest which must vest within a life in being and 21 years thereafter was valid; any interest which might vest at a period more remote was invalid. Note that this Rule had nothing to do with the potential duration of the interest. It was concerned only with the time at which a certain interest should be vested in some person who could alienate it.

Sec. 206. Executory Interests—Statute of Uses in the United States. In the United States, the Statute of Uses has been substantially re-enacted in some jurisdictions. In others, the statute was adopted as part of the common law. There are, however, several jurisdictions, in which, owing either to direct decisions or to particular statutory provisions, the statute cannot be regarded as being in force.

Sec. 207. Executory Interests—Statutory Provisions as to Creation of Executory Interests in the United States. Statutes in many jurisdictions allow the creation of a future estate of freehold, with or without a precedent estate, either by deed or by will. As Tiffany points out,[32] that type of statutory provision dispenses with the necessity of a particular estate to support the executory limitation, and would seem to have the further effect of preventing the possibility of the failure of a limitation under the rule that a contingent remainder must vest before the termination of the preceding estate. Statutes in several states undertake to assimilate contingent

---

[32] Tiffany, The Law of Real Property (2d ed. 1929), Vol. I, secs. 177, 178, pp. 590, 591.

remainders to executory interests. Sometimes such statutes are to the effect that any contingent remainder will be valid if it would be valid as a conditional limitation. Other statutes provide that any estate which would be good by way of executory devise is equally good if created by deed.

Sec. 208. Executory Interests—Creation of Executory Interests in Those Jurisdictions of the United States where the Statute of Uses is not in Force, and where there is no Statute Allowing the Creation of Future Estates. It has been held in a few states, although the Statute of Uses is not in force, and there is no statute allowing the creation of future estates, that interests involving a right of future possession may be created without reference to the rules of common law.

Sec. 209. Executory Interests—Conveyances at Common Law. According to the common law, which regarded an executory interest whether created by will or by deed, as being merely a possibility, rather than an estate in the land, such executory interest could not be transferred by conveyance *inter vivos*. It could, however, be released to the holder of the land. In addition, assignment of such an interest has always been permitted in equity, and it was also possible to transfer by a conveyance which would create an estoppel against the grantor.

Sec. 210. Executory Interests—Conveyances in the United States.[33] At the present day, over half of the states have statutes declaring the transferability of interests in the land. Some of these statutes expressly declare that executory interests are freely transferable. A like result is reached by construction of some of the others. Equity will recognize the transfer of such an interest, if made for a good or valuable consideration. Transferability by estoppel has also been applied to deeds executed by persons having executory interests. In only a few of the states have courts allowed the free transferability of executory interests without the excuse of a statute. In five states remnants of the early common law prohibi-

---

[33] American Law Institute, Restatement of Property. Tentative Draft Number 4, pp. 134-135.

tion against the free alienability of executory interests survive.

Sec. 211. Executory Interests—Devolution on Death at Common Law. The common law principles noted in the discussion of reversions, of descent being "cast" on the heir and the heir's taking by "descent" or "taking by representation" applied equally to executory interests.

Like contingent remainders, executory interests were not devisable originally, but as in the case of contingent remainders, the common law finally recognized their devisability.

Sec. 212. Executory Interests—Devolution on Death in the United States.[34] In the case of executory interests, there seems to be at the present day in the United States, general agreement that the persons taking such interests in the event of an intestacy are determined upon the occurrence of the intestacy in the same way as in the case of possessory ownership. The person upon whom descent is cast can constitute a new stock of descent; there is no longer a principle of "descent" or "taking by representation." The doctrine of the English common law has been abolished almost universally by the descent and distribution statutes of the states.

In all jurisdictions there are statutes defining the sorts of interests that are devisable. There is one group of states in which the statute provides that any interest which is descendible is devisable. Another group has statutes providing that "expectant estates" are devisable. The largest group has statutes that provide for the devisability of "lands or interests therein."

b. Powers of Appointment

Sec. 213. Powers of Appointment at Common Law. We have already mentioned that during the Middle Ages in a few localities there was a custom which permitted a testator to

---

[34] American Law Institute, Restatement of Property, Tentative Draft Number 4, 134-138. Proposed Final Draft, 343.

devise his land. Where such a custom prevailed, it was possible for the testator by his will to give his executor a power to sell the land, without giving him an estate in the land. Since the executor had no estate in the land, but only a bare power, he could bargain and sell the land to a purchaser, without the necessity of making entry upon the land. The purchaser, of course, acquired the right to enter. Even before the enactment of the Statute of Uses the capacity to create powers had been extended by the rise of uses and the fact that it was possible for testators either to give their feoffees to uses power to convey or to give any third person power to direct their feoffees to uses to convey. The Statute of Uses operated to transform the estates, created through the exercise of the power, into legal estates. Before the statute, it had been possible for the grantor to uses either to reserve to himself the power to revoke the old uses and declare new ones, or to give that power to a third person. Once the new uses had been declared, the feoffees to uses became trustees for the new beneficiaries. This was utilized for the purpose of making jointures, leases, exchanges or sales. The creation of a power of appointment was a common mode of calling into operation the Statute of Uses. Such a power was created by giving a person, regardless of whether or not he had an interest in the land, power of disposing of an interest. The "donor" of the power of appointment conveyed the land to a feoffee by means of a conveyance operative at common law. At the time of the conveyance, he stated that certain uses were to arise upon the execution of the proper instrument by a designated person. When that person executed the instrument, the instrument operated as an appointment. It should be noted that the "donor" or original settlor, was the person from whom the appointee received his estate, rather than the person who had executed the instrument which had operated as an appointment. It was simply a case of the original settlor choosing to leave the declaration of the uses to a third person to be made later rather than declaring the uses at the time of making the conveyance.

Sec. 214. Powers of Appointment—Effect of the Statute of Wills. After the passage of the Statute of Wills, it was possible for testators as well as settlors to avail themselves of the machinery of the Statute of Uses. By their wills they were able to create powers which acted on a declaration of a use upon the seisin of the holder of the legal title.

Sec. 215. Powers of Appointment in the United States. In the United States powers of appointment have apparently always existed and been exercised. From time to time, they have been particularly useful in enabling a testator to avoid an inheritance tax statute.

c. Uses not Executed by the Statute of Uses

Sec. 216. Uses not Executed by the Statute of Uses. It is clear from the words of the Statute of Uses that it was not the intention, in enacting that statute, to abolish uses. The statute did not purport to apply to all uses. The first clause dealt only with the case where one person was *seised* to the use of another. At the time of the enactment of the statute, seisin was applicable only in the case of hereditaments. Seisin had no application where one person was possessed of a chattel either real or personal to the use of another. The statute applied where one person was seised to the use of another for a term of years, but not where one was possessed of a term of years to the use of another. Again, the statute had application only to those cases where the person seised to the use of another was merely under the passive duty of allowing the person who had the use to occupy the land for the estate limited to him. Where the feoffee, on the other hand, had active duties to perform, the statute did not apply. It is clear that in that case no evils arose from the division of ownership. Had the legal title been taken from the feoffee who had active duties to perform, it would have become impossible for him to carry out the terms of the trust.

After the Statute of Uses had been in effect for about a century, the courts decided that by the terms of the statute, it applied only to one use. Consequently, if A conveyed to B to the use of C to the use of D, the statute executed only the first use to C, so that C held the legal title for the use of D. This was spoken of as a "use upon a use," and led to a remark by an eminent judge that the only effect of the Statute of Uses had been to add three words to a conveyance.

Thus, even after the Statute of Uses, there were three types of uses to which the statute did not apply, and under which there was still the separation of legal and equitable title, viz., trust terms, active uses and uses upon uses. These developed into the modern law of trusts.

The courts of the United States followed the English courts from the beginning in omitting all three types of uses from the operation of the statute.

BIBLIOGRAPHY

Material on Estates in Fee Simple.

American Law Institute, Proposed Final Draft, Restatement of Property (1936), 98-101, 112-113, 115-126.

2 Bl. Comm. c. VII * 104-109; c. XIV * 200-234.

Digby, Kenelm Edward, An Introduction to the History of Real Property (5th ed. 1897), 95-100, 144-152, 315-357.

Holdsworth, W. S., An Historical Introduction to the Land Law (1927), 48-55, 77-85, 110-116, 140-166, 291-295.

Holdsworth, W. S., A History of English Law (3d ed. 1931), Vol. III, 105-107, 217-234; Vol. IV, 407-473; Vol. VII, 356-362.

Plucknett, Theodore T. F., A Concise History of the Common Law (1929), 309-317, 320-345.

Pollock and Maitland, The History of English Law Before the Time of Edward I (2d ed. 1911), Vol. II, 82-105, 253-311.

Tiffany, The Law of Real Property (2d ed. 1929), Vol. II, secs. 427-430, 487-493.

Material on the Maritagium.

Holdsworth, W. S., A History of English Law (3d ed. 1931), Vol. III, 111-112.

Plucknett, Theodore T. F., A Concise History of the Common Law (1929), 346-348.

Pollock and Maitland, The History of English Law Before the Time of Edward I (2d ed. 1911), Vol. II, 15-17.

Material on Conditional Fees Simple.

American Law Institute, Proposed Final Draft, Restatement of Property (1936), 195-213.

2 Bl. Comm. c. VII * 110, 111.

Digby, Kenelm Edward, An Introduction to the History of the Law of Real Property (5th ed. 1897), 161-174.

Holdsworth, W. S., A History of English Law (3d ed. 1931), Vol. III, 111-114.

Plucknett, Theodore T. F., A Concise History of the Common Law (1929), 348-351.

Pollock and Maitland, The History of English Law Before the Time of Edward I (2d ed. 1911), Vol. II, 17-19.

Material on Estates in Fee Tail.

American Law Institute, Tentative Draft Number 2, Restatement of Property, 89, 90. Proposed Final Draft (1936), 196-206, 221.

2 Bl. Comm. c. VII *112-119.

Digby, Kenelm Edward, An Introduction to the History of the Law of Real Property (5th ed. 1897), 105-108, 222-230, 249-258.

Holdsworth, W. S., An Historical Introduction to the Land Law (1927), 55-59, 116-118.

Holdsworth, W. S., A History of English Law (3d ed. 1931), Vol. III, 114-120, 234-246.

Morris, R. B., Primogeniture and Entailed Estates in America, (1927) 27 Col. L. Rev. 24.

Plucknett, Theodore T. F., A Concise History of the Common Law (1929), 351-357.

Pollock and Maitland, The History of English Law Before the Time of Edward I (2d ed. 1911), Vol. II, 100-105.

Riddell, The Fine in England, the United States and Canada, (1923) 11 Minn. L. Rev. 220.

Tiffany, The Law of Real Property (2d ed. 1929), Vol. II, sec. 427.

Material on Life Estates.

2 Bl. Comm. c. VIII *120-136.

Digby, Kenelm Edward, An Introduction to the History of the Law of Real Property (5th ed. 1897), 127-130, 174-176.

Holdsworth, W. S., An Historical Introduction to the Land Law (1927), 60-63, 87-89.

Holdsworth, W. S., A History of English Law (3d ed. 1931), Vol. III, 120-125, 185-197.

Tiffany, The Law of Real Property (2d ed. 1929), Vol. I, secs. 266-272.

Material on Non-Freehold Interests.

2 Bl. Comm. c. VII, IX * 140-150.

Digby, Kenelm Edward, An Introduction to the History of the Law of Real Property (5th ed. 1897), 176-181, 241-249, 413-416.

Holdsworth, W. S., An Historical Introduction to the Land Law (1927), 63-65, 71-73, 120, 230-255.

Holdsworth, W. S., A History of English Law (3d ed. 1931), Vol. III, 125, 213-217, 248-249; Vol. VII, 238-250.

Pollock and Maitland, The History of English Law Before the Time of Edward I (2d ed. 1911), Vol. II, 105-117.

Tiffany, The Law of Real Property (2d ed. 1929), Vol. I, sec. 42.

Tiffany, Landlord and Tenant (1910), Vol. II, secs. 13, 14, 15, 109, 113, 119, 165 ff.

Material on Rights of Re-entry.

American Law Institute, Proposed Final Draft, Restatement of Property (1936), 328, 329, 343. Tentative Draft Number 4, 112-122.

Material on Possibility of Reverter.

American Law Institute, Proposed Final Draft, Restatement of Property (1936), 326, 327, 343. Tentative Draft Number 4, 107-112.

Material on Reversions.

2 Bl. Comm. c. XI * 175, 176.

Digby, Kenelm Edward, An Introduction to the History of the Law of Real Property (5th ed. 1897), 259-262.

Holdsworth, W. S., An Historical Introduction to the Land Law (1927), 65-67.

Holdsworth, W. S., A History of English Law (3d ed. 1931), Vol. III, 132-133.

Pollock and Maitland, The History of English Law Before the Time of Edward I (2d ed. 1911), Vol. II, 21-22.

Tiffany, The Law of Real Property (2d ed. 1929), Vol. I, sec. 290.

Material on Remainders.

American Law Institute, Proposed Final Draft, Restatement of Property (1936), 326, 331-340.

2 Bl. Comm. c. XI * 163-168.

Digby, Kenelm Edward, An Introduction to the History of the Law of Real Property (5th ed. 1897), 262-265.

Holdsworth, W. S., An Historical Introduction to the Land Law (1927), 67-68.

Holdsworth, W. S., A History of English Law (3d ed. 1931), Vol. III, 134-135.

Tiffany, The Law of Real Property (2d ed. 1929), Vol. I, sec. 290.

Material on Contingent Remainders.

American Law Institute, Proposed Final Draft, Restatement of Property (1936), 326, 327, 331-340.

2 Bl. Comm. c. XI * 168, 169.

Digby, Kenelm Edward, An Introduction to the History of the Law of Real Property (5th ed. 1897), 266-275.

Holdsworth, W. S., An Historical Introduction to the Land Law (1927), 187-197.

Holdsworth, W. S., A History of English Law (3d ed. 1931), Vol. III, 135-137; Vol. VII, 81-116.

Tiffany, The Law of Real Property (2d ed. 1929), Vol. I, sec. 290.

Material on Executory Interests.

American Law Institute, Proposed Final Draft, Restatement of Property (1936), 326, 327, 331-340.

2 Bl. Comm. c. XI * 173-175.

Digby, Kenelm Edward, An Introduction to the History of the Law of Real Property (5th ed. 1897), 357-389.

Holdsworth, W. S., An Historical Introduction to the Land Law (1927), 197-230.

Holdsworth, W. S., A History of English Law (3d ed. 1931), Vol. VII, 116-238.

Tiffany, The Law of Real Property (2d ed. 1929), Vol. I, secs. 177-178.

CHAPTER III

SEISIN, THE REAL ACTIONS AND ADVERSE POSSESSION

Sec. 217. Seisin at Common Law. Originally seisin and possession were used as interchangeable terms in the English law of real property. Seisin had the same root as the German *"Besitz";* it connoted peaceful enjoyment of the land, having nothing to do with the word seize, or take by violence. This idea is well expressed in the words of Coke:[1] ". . . till he hath seisin, all is *labor et dolor et vexatio spiritus,* but when he has obtained seisin he may *sedere et acquiescere."* Gradually, however, seisin was distinguished from possession, in time coming to be used to describe only the possession of those who had freehold estates in the land, while the word "possession" was used in respect to chattels real and personal.

The royal remedies given by Henry II, during the second half of the twelfth century, for the protection of seisin, were available only to those who were seised of a free tenement. The tenant in fee simple, the tenant in fee tail and the life tenant were all seised of such a free tenement, but the tenant for years was not, merely having possession of a chattel real. Where a lord who held land in fee by one of the free tenures granted that land to another to be held in fee by a free tenure, both the lord and the tenant were said to be seised, the lord

---

[1] 6 Co. Rep. 57 b.

being seised in service and the tenant being seised in demesne. The reversioner likewise was seized of the land in service, and the particular tenant was seised in demesne. Originally, on the other hand, the remainderman had no seisin.

The early common law then made no such distinction between possession and ownership, as is drawn at the present day. Today possession in our system is understood as denoting physical control over a thing with the intention of controlling that thing; the possessor may or may not be the owner. We regard ownership as the relation of the person to the thing, by virtue of which relationship the person has certain rights enforceable at law against all persons generally with reference to the thing.

The early common law of England concerned itself with the development and maintenance of rules for the settlement of disputes concerning the possession of land, the immediate question being the determination of the dispute between the man actually in possession of the land, and the one who insisted that he was entitled to possession. The early law favored the actual occupier of the land, regarding him as the possessor as opposed to the man who disputed such an occupier's right. In the twelfth and thirteenth centuries the common law took the point of view that if the possession of an actual occupier of the land were questioned, the burden rested on the plaintiff to prove his case.

Sec. 218. Real Actions at Common Law—Varieties. There were three main groups of real actions available to a person who wished to assert a right to a freehold interest in land held by one of the free tenures: (1) The writs of right; (2) the possessory assizes of *novel disseisin* and *mort d'ancestor;* and (3) the writs of entry *sur disseisin.*

During the reign of Henry II the principle seems to have become established that no man need answer for his freehold without royal writ. That meant that it was only where an action was begun by royal writ that an answer need be made. It did not mean that all litigation concerning freeholds must be brought in the royal courts.

Sec. 219. Real Actions at Common Law—Writs of Right —Distinction Between Writ of Right Patent and Praecipe in Capite. The writs of right dealt not only with seisin but with the right as between the two parties; they were proprietary, as opposed to possessory, actions. They fell into two main classes: (1) The writ of right patent; and (2) the *praecipe in capite.*

The writ of right patent, so called because it was an open, not a sealed writ, was used where the land was held of one other than the king, that is, of a *mesne* lord. This writ recognized that the matter was within the jurisdiction of the lord, rather than of the king. The writ was directed by the king to the lord, informing him that one of his tenants had complained that justice was denied him in the lord's court, and ordering the lord to see that right was done to the tenant, or the king himself would take the matter up. It should be noted that this writ did not in the first instance institute litigation. Only in the event that the lord failed to obey the command of the king, was resort to litigation necessary.

The writ *praecipe in capite* was properly used where the land was held in chief of the king. The writ was then directed to the sheriff instructing him to order the occupier to restore the land to the demandant, and if the occupier failed to obey, to summon him to give the reasons for such failure. The proceedings took place in the king's court. Henry II, in the course of his expansion of the royal power at the expense of the lords, extended the use of this writ to cases where the land was held not in chief of the king but of a *mesne* lord. This extension was checked by section 34 of Magna Carta in 1217. That section provided that in the future the writ called *praecipe* should not issue in such a way as to deprive a free man of his court. The result of this provision was that it was possible to stop an action which had been begun by the writ *praecipe in capite,* even at its final stage, by showing that the land was not held of the king in chief.

In these actions the question involved was that of a better right as between the demandant and the defendant.

The demandant appeared and claimed the land, alleging seisin either of himself or of his ancestor, "as of right," at some period within the existing statute of limitations. He offered battle through a champion, who testified to the demandant's seisin. Until 1189, when Henry II gave the defendant the privilege of choosing between trial by battle and trial by the Grand Assize, the method of trial was always by battle. The Grand Assize was a group of twelve knights of the neighborhood, who had been chosen by four other knights of the neighborhood. The twelve were sworn to "recognize" whether the demandant or the defendant had the greater right to the land.

Since the question to be settled was only as to which of the two parties had the better right to the land, the right of a third person, through whom the defendant did not claim, could not be introduced to defeat the claim of the demandant, since a third person's right was irrelevant in the determination of the question of right as between the two parties. Likewise the judgment in the action bound only the two parties. A stranger was bound only if, being under no disability, he failed to advance his claim within a year and a day of the execution of the judgment.

These actions had fallen into popular disfavor by the end of the thirteenth century. They were cumbersome and slow. Manifold delays were allowed and the procedure was dilatory in the extreme.

Sec. 220. Real Actions at Common Law—Possessory Assize of Novel Disseisin. The distinctly possessory assize of *novel disseisin* was another remedy that was in common use during the twelfth and thirteenth centuries. Disseisin was the word used to describe the turning the tenant out of his fee and usurping his place. The usurper was spoken of as the disseisor; the man turned out of possession was called the disseisee. The assize of *novel disseisin* was the possessory remedy available where a demandant asserted that he had been recently turned out of possession by one who had disseised him without right. This assize was founded on a royal ordinance of about 1166. The writ directed the sheriff to summon twelve men to answer the question whether the defendant had unjustly and without judgment disseised the demandant of his free tenement, since some recent date, for instance, since the king's last voyage to Normandy. The action could proceed even in the absence of appearance and plea by the defendant; if he did not appear, judgment went by default. No pleadings were necessary since the question for the twelve men had been formulated in advance of the defendant's appearance. No pleas of a proprietary nature were allowed, since the action was entirely possessory. It must be noted that this assize protected a *de facto* seisin, without any regard to the question as to whether the seisin were rightful or wrongful. It did not decide the question of right as between the two parties; if the unsuccessful party wished to have that question litigated, he could, after the judgment of the assize had gone against him, have recourse to the proprietary action, the writ of right.

The man who was disseised, if he wished to avail himself of the remedy by assize of *novel disseisin,* instead of having recourse to the writ of right, had to take steps within four days if the disseisor were actually on the land. After four days, at early law, the disseisor acquired seisin.

The assize could be brought not only against the disseisor himself but also against his feoffee if he had alienated the land, or against anyone who had dispossessed the original disseisor.

After the thirteenth century, however, this action too declined in popular favor. The law had grown more elaborate, and the number of incidental questions that had to be answered by the jury before they reached the determination of the main question, had become very large. Moreover, it had become possible to introduce special pleas, or *"exceptiones,"* thus giving greater scope to the art of the pleader.

The action was limited in that it could be brought against the disseisor's alienee only during the lifetime of the disseisor, nor could it be brought, even during the lifetime of the disseisor, against any other than the first person to whom the disseisor had conveyed the land. There was, in addition, a growing tendency to introduce considerations of title in this action. By the Statute of Westminster II, the availability of the assize was extended to an owner as against a tenant for years or a guardian who had made a tortious conveyance of the fee, and also against their feoffees. Under such circumstances, the demandant could recover against persons who had peaceable seisin, on the basis of the strength of his title.

Originally the requirement had been that the disseisin be "novel" or recent. The period of limitation, however, gradually lengthened. At first short periods had been fixed by royal ordinance, but in time such periods ceased to be fixed. The Statute of Westminster fixed 1242 as the date back of which a disseisin could not be alleged, and that date remained unchanged until 1540. The plaintiff thus naturally came to rely increasingly on title.

Sec. 221. Real Actions at Common Law—Possessory Assize of Mort D'Ancestor. The assize of *novel disseisin* was not available to the heir of one who had died seised, since that heir had never acquired seisin himself. He was, however, protected by the assize of *mort d'ancestor* established by royal ordinance about 1176. This assize was the possessory remedy used by the heir of one who had died seised of a free tenement, whereupon another, called an abator, had forestalled the heir and entered upon the vacant tenement. The demandant asserted that within some recent time fixed by ordinance, the one whose heir he was had died seised of the tenement. The questions for the assize to answer were whether M, the father, mother, brother, sister, uncle or aunt of A, the demandant, had been seised in his demesne as of fee of the land in question now held by X, whether M had died within the time limited for bringing the action and whether A was M's next heir. It must be noted that it was not sufficient that the demandant was the ancestor's next heir; it was necessary that there be a very close relationship between the demandant and the deceased. The allegation of the demandant was of seisin "as of fee," but it was not necessary, as was required in a writ of right, that seisin "as of right" be alleged. Therefore the defendant was not allowed to urge pleas of a proprietary nature.

In this action, again, the questions were answered by twelve men of the neighborhood summoned for that purpose. Here again, even in the absence of appearance and plea by the defendant, the plaintiff could get judgment.

The assize was available against anyone holding the land, no matter how remote from the original disseisor, and regardless of good faith on the part of the occupier of the land. The heir might recover possession by this action even as against one who held the land by virtue of a purchase in good faith from the disseisor, or by inheritance.

Sec. 222. Real Actions at Common Law—Writs of Entry. The final group of real actions to be considered is the group of writs called the writs of entry, which were halfway between the proprietary writs of right and the possessory assizes. The reasons that led to the invention of these writs were that the older writs of right were very slow, and the scope of the assize of *novel disseisin* limited. To force a man who might have had long-continued and recent seisin to prove his title by means of the cumbersome writ of right was considered too great a hardship. The result of this feeling was the evolution of writs of entry *sur disseisin*. A writ of entry for the disseisee against the heir of the disseisor was made a writ of course in the year 1205, followed soon after by a writ for the heir of the disseisee. At first it seems that this remedy was resorted to only where the death of one of the parties had put an end to the action by assize of *novel disseisin*. The writ of entry ordered the tenant to give up the land or to answer the demandant's claim, adding a suggestion of some recent flaw in the tenant's title. All of the new writs had the common feature of alleging that the defendant had no entry upon the land except in a way which could not give him a good title. The question to be tried was whether or not the defendant had come to his possession in the manner asserted by the demandant.

Originally, it was not possible to allege a faulty entry at any time in the past, however remote, but this was changed by the Statute of Marlborough in 1267. That statute provided that a flaw in the tenant's title might be alleged at any time in the past.

There was a great variety of writs of entry, and these writs superseded both the writs of right and the possessory assizes. However, due to the fact that there was a different type of writ for practically every situation, it was of great importance that the demandant choose the particular writ applicable to his case. Minute verbal accuracy was required in the pleadings, and the rules governing pleading had become very precise. The process in these actions was long and complicated.

Sec. 223. Action of Ejectment. Because of the defects inherent in the old real actions, freeholders developed a method of making the action of ejectment, originally designed for the non-freeholder, the tenant for years, available to them. The action of ejectment was an action of trespass and thus speedy as compared with the real actions. The form of action was always the same, another point of superiority over the numerous writs that were so narrow in scope. Moreover, the verbal accuracy required in the writs of entry was not demanded in the action of ejectment; nor were the strict rules of pleading applicable to that action.

Since the action was available only to tenants for years, the freeholder initiated the action by the creation of a term for years. The person who was claiming the land entered upon the land, and there executed a lease leaving his lessee in possession. Then, instead of waiting for the lessee to be ejected by the actual tenant who was occupying the land, the claimant arranged for a third person, totally unconnected with the land, who was termed the "casual ejector," to eject the lessee. This meant that the lessee was then in a position to bring an action of ejectment. It was not long before the courts held that the plaintiff could not recover the land against the casual ejector without giving the actual tenant notice of the action so that he might intervene if he wished to do so. The plaintiff was required to prove four things: (1) The lease under which he claimed; (2) his entry under that lease; (3) his ouster by the defendant; and (4) the title of his lessor to make the lease. The last element of course was the essential part of the plaintiff's case, since it was there that the question of title to the freehold was involved.

By the time of the Commonwealth, in the middle of the seventeenth century, the point had been reached where the lease, entry and ouster had all become fictitious. As soon as the action was started, the casual ejector notified the real tenant that such an action had been brought against him, and that he did not intend to enter any defense. The tenant, who was of course the real party in interest, was allowed to intervene as party defendant on the condition that he admitted the fictitious lease, entry and ouster. This meant that the real point at issue was the only one to be tried on the merits, namely, the question of title to the freehold. If the tenant after having been made defendant, failed to appear and admit the lease, entry and ouster, the plaintiff was non-suited, since under those circumstances he was unable to prove the entry, lease and ouster. However, he was still able to obtain judgment against the casual ejector, whereupon the tenant would be dispossessed. If the tenant actually appeared and admitted the lease, entry and ouster, the case was then tried on the merits so far as the title was concerned.

At first there was some feeling that since the defendant might be in danger of losing his costs if the lessee were not a real person, the lessee must be a real person. The lessee, of course, was only the nominal plaintiff, which meant that even his death did not interrupt the action. The difficulty as to costs was solved by making the real party at interest, the plaintiff's lessor, undertake to pay costs in the event of the judgment being in favor of the defendant. It became customary to use entirely fictitious parties, the lessee being termed John Doe, and the casual ejector Richard Roe.

Sec. 224. Action of Ejectment—Result of Judgment in Action of Ejectment. There was one point as to which the old real actions were superior to the newer action of ejectment which superseded them. They settled the question of right as between the parties with finality, which was not true of the action of ejectment. Ejectment, it must be remembered, was an action of trespass, with the result that the only thing that was settled by an action of ejectment was that the defendant had not been guilty of the particular trespass of which he was accused. That meant that the verdict in one action of ejectment did not constitute a bar to another action of ejectment for a different trespass.

The court of Chancery was the first to take action towards remedying this situation. In the earlier half of the seventeenth century, that court gave injunctive relief against persons who brought repeated actions of ejectment to try the same title. The House of Lords at the beginning of the eighteenth century upheld such injunctions.

In the second half of the seventeenth century, the courts of law refused to permit a second action between the same parties until the costs of the first action had been paid. In the following century, they would not allow a second action, regardless of whether the parties were the same, until the costs of the first had been paid.

It was finally decided that it was necessary for the plaintiff in an action of ejectment to show an absolutely good title, which meant that the right of a third person constituted a good defense to the action.

Sec. 225. Real Actions in the United States.[2] At the time when the first colonies were established in America, the action of ejectment had already superseded the real actions as a method of trying title. In New England, due to a dislike of the use of fictions, an action on the case was made use

---

[2] Bordwell, Seisin and Disseisin, (1921) 34 Harv. L. Rev. 725.

of for the recovery of land. Later, writs of entry were used in Massachusetts and New Hampshire, and in Connecticut the writ of disseisin was used. In Massachusetts, following the Revolution, there was an effort to reintroduce the old writs of entry, but that attempt failed, and instead a single statutory writ was established. In Connecticut, the writ of disseisin was employed rather than writs of right, writs of entry or the action of ejectment, which served to keep alive the old terminology. The action, itself, however, rather resembled ejectment stripped of its fictions than one of the old real actions used during the Middle Ages.

Outside of New England, it seems that the action of ejectment was used, the old real actions not being employed. The same difficulty was found in the fact that the verdict in that action was not conclusive. That defect was finally cured in most jurisdictions by statute.

Sec. 226. Position of Disseisor and Disseisee at Common Law—Position of the Disseisor. In the thirteenth century in England, unless the disseisee asserted his right of entry against the disseisor within a very limited time, no more than three or four days, by assize of *novel disseisin,* he had thereafter to fall back upon the right of action by writ of right or writ of entry. After four days had elapsed, the disseisor had gained seisin, tortious, but still seisin, and with it all of the rights to property accorded by seisin. He could alienate his interest; his wife was entitled to dower at his death; his heir inherited the land; the rights appendant to the estate belonged to him. Similarly, if he were the husband of a woman who had tortious seisin, he was entitled, at her death, to curtesy. He was affected by the incidents of tenure just as though his seisin had been rightfully acquired.

Sec. 227. Position of the Disseisee at Common Law. On the other hand, the one disseised had lost all power of dealing with the property, as a result of his loss of seisin. He had no interest in the land that he could alienate to a third person. To be sure, he had a right of action, but that right of action remained inalienable until 1845. At his death, his wife was not entitled to dower; the only right that passed to his heir was a right of action. He was no longer liable to the incidents of tenure. Likewise, the husband of a woman disseised had no right to curtesy.

Sec. 228. Change in the Position of the Disseisee as Against the Disseisor—Extension of the Disseisee's Right of Entry. In the course of time, the old idea that the rights of the disseisor prevailed even against the true owner unless the latter immediately asserted his rights of entry, suffered modification, but the idea persisted that as against the world at large, that is, as against every one other than the true owner, the disseisor had all the rights of the true owner. The change in attitude towards the disseisee as against the disseisor was responsible for many rather difficult doctrines of law that came to prevail.

Originally, in the thirteenth century, any extension of the three or four days within which the disseisee could enter upon the disseisor and assert his right of entry by the assize of *novel disseisin* was regarded as exceptional. By the time of Littleton, towards the close of the fifteenth century, it had come to be felt that any fettering of the true owner's right to enter was exceptional. One of the factors that operated to bring about this change in attitude was the fact that the period within which the right of entry could be asserted was lengthened due to the neglect to pass any statutes of limitation. At first royal ordinances had established short periods of limitation of the time within which the assize of *novel disseisin* must be brought, but the last such period was fixed during the reign of Edward I, by Statute of Westminster I at 1242, and no change was made until 1540. This meant of course that the plaintiff gradually came to rely increasingly on title.

During the same period it came to be thought that the length of time within which the disseisee could assert his right of entry was a matter for judicial discretion, and the judges displayed a tendency to favor the disseisee as against the disseisor. It was held that the right to enter upon the disseisor should be extended to the right to enter upon the person to whom the disseisor conveyed the land, since otherwise every disseisor would have it within his power to defeat the disseisee's right of entry simply by conveying to a third person. Towards the close of the thirteenth century, a statute was enacted providing that if a lessee for years or a guardian made a conveyance in fee, not only were the lessee for years and the guardian themselves to be treated as disseisors, but also their alienees. That meant that the disseisee could enter upon such persons and bring an assize against them.

Sec. 229. **Survival of Limitations upon the Disseisee's Right of Entry—Doctrine of "Descent Cast."** There were, however, two notable survivals of the old ideas of the limitations of the disseisee's rights as against the disseisor. The first of these arose where the disseisor had died, and his heir had entered. Under such circumstances, the disseisee lost his right of entry and thereafter had to have recourse to his right of action. This was spoken of as the tolling, or taking away, of the disseisee's right of entry by descent cast on the disseisee's heir. It was, however, possible to prevent this result following the casting of descent on the heir, if the disseisee, being unable to enter, had made continual claim.

Sec. 230. **Survival of Limitations upon the Disseisee's Right of Entry—The Doctrine of Discontinuance.** The second survival of the limitations of the disseisee's right of entry was known as the doctrine of discontinuance. If A, a husband seised in right of his wife, or a clergyman seised in right of his religious order, or a tenant in tail, conveyed to B, a third person, and then died, the person who was entitled to enter upon the termination of A's interest lost that right of entry and was relegated to a right of action against B. It was said that a discontinuance or devesting of the estate had resulted from A's conveyance.

Sec. 231. **Statutory Modifications in Favor of the Disseisee.** Towards the end of the fifteenth century, and during the course of the sixteenth century, statutes were enacted that altered the position of the disseisee as against the disseissor in certain respects. A dowress was prevented from working a discontinuance by a statute of 1495; in 1540 a wife and her heirs were given the right of entry, notwithstanding an alienation by the husband. The latter statute was superseded by one enacted in 1572 which provided that recoveries suffered by tenants for life and other limited owners should be void. That statute was construed to mean that suffering the recovery brought about a forfeiture so that the person next entitled thereupon had the right of entry. In 1540 the doctrine of descent cast was modified by a statute providing that descent cast should not operate to take away the disseisee's right of entry, unless the disseisor had had peaceable possession for five years, without continual claim having been made by the disseisee.

Sec. 232. Change in Judicial Attitude Towards the Element of Good Faith. During the greater part of the Middle Ages, no emphasis had been placed by the courts upon the good faith of parties to a conveyance, but a change in that attitude took place in the sixteenth century. The judges then began to direct their attention towards the existence or absence of good faith on the part of the parties.

Sec. 233. Change in the Position of the Disseisee as to Liability to Certain Tenurial Incidents. We have already mentioned the fact that originally the incidents of tenure attached to the estate of the disseisor, and not to the disseisee's right of entry or of action. From about the middle of the fourteenth century, there was a change in the common law rules regarding certain of the profitable tenurial incidents. During the reign of Edward III, it was held that upon the death of the disseisee without heirs his lord was entitled to enter upon the disseisor and retake the land by virtue of the operation of the right to escheat. Later, during the reign of Henry VI, it was also held that on the death of the disseisee leaving a minor heir, the lord of the disseisee was entitled to wardship of the heir. Thus it came to be felt that the disseisee, while still out of possession, had something that could be made the basis of a claim by a third person, which meant that the disseisee still had something partaking of the nature of a property right.

Sec. 234. Effect of the Statute of Uses on the Concept of Seisin. Another factor that must be taken into account concerning the change in attitude towards the disseisee as opposed to the disseisor was that the seisin acquired by virtue of the operation of the Statute of Uses was a different sort of seisin from that during the thirteenth century, in so far as it had lost its connection with physical control. Seisin acquired by a conveyance operating under the Statute of Uses was acquired without transmutation of possession. By the year 1666, the courts had come to distinguish between the seisin acquired by the effect of the statute and the physical control necessary to maintain an action for trespass. This too helped to strengthen the tendency that was developing to connect seisin with title.

Sec. 235. Development of the Doctrine of Disseisin at Election. One of the most important factors in this connection, however, was the development of the doctrine of disseisin at election. In its original form that doctrine was applicable where a tenant, under pressure from some person other than the lord to whom the rent was payable, had paid the rent to that other person. The lord thereupon had a choice between considering himself disseised by the improper action on the part of his tenant, and bringing an assize against the man who had compelled the tenant to pay, and of bringing an action against the tenant for the rent due and unpaid, since of course payment to a person who had not been entitled to receive the rent had not had the effect of discharging the tenant's obligation to the lord. In the event of the lord's pursuing the latter course, he had elected to treat himself as not having been disseised.

During the course of the sixteenth and seventeenth centuries the scope of the doctrine of disseisin at election was extended to corporeal hereditaments.

In the case where a man died leaving two sons, and the younger entered, and died leaving issue, and the issue entered, the elder brother could still, in spite of the fact the descent had been cast on the younger brother's heir, enter upon him. In this situation the same result was reached as would have been reached by applying the principle upon which the doc-. trine of disseisin at election was based. In spite of the fact that descent had been cast on the heir, the elder brother was treated as being in the same position he would have been in, had descent not been cast on the heir. Another analogous situation existed where an infant had executed a contract; in the course of the seventeenth century it was held that such a contract was voidable at the option of the infant.

Another class of cases in which the doctrine of disseisin at election was extended were those cases where a freeholder had leased his land to a copyholder or to a tenant for years, and the copyholder or the tenant for years had made a conveyance which the interest he held did not warrant him in making. In so doing, though, it was quite possible that he had acted without any intention of disseising the freeholder. Under those circumstances, it was held that the freeholder could either consider himself not disseised, and continue to treat the copyholder or tenant for years as his tenant, or he might bring an assize against the feoffee, thus indicating that he considered that he had been disseised by the conveyance. In this type of case stress was placed on the intention of the parties.

As Holdsworth [3] points out, the doctrine of disseisin at election was the most efficacious of all the modifications of the law designed to improve the position of the true owner. The other modifications had gone on the principle of extending the right of entry of the disseisee or his right of action to recover the seisin. The doctrine of disseisin at election, however, had the effect of increasing the powers of the disseisee, while still disseised, in dealing with the property, since a person who was disseised only at his own option was disseised

---

[3] Holdsworth, W. S., A History of English Law (3d ed. 1931), Vol. VII, 41-42.

only for the single purpose of his right to bring an assize, and not for any other purpose.

In spite of all the changes that had occurred in the attitude of the courts regarding the position of the disseisee as against the disseisor, it was still true that as against the world at large the disseisor, with the exception of one who was so regarded only at the election of the true owner, was treated as the person who had the rights of property.

Sec. 236. Statutory Modifications in Favor of the Disseisor. There were also various statutes that operated in favor of the disseisor as against the disseisee: the statute of 1540 which forbade the sale of lands by owners out of possession, Henry VII's Statute of Fines and the statutes of limitation passed during the reigns of Henry VIII and James I. The Statute of Fines made a fine levied with proclamation a bar to adverse claims after five years had elapsed. Henry VIII's Statute of Limitations established certain periods of limitation for the different classes of real actions and provided that after the expiration of such periods those disseised were thereafter barred from asserting their claims. The Statute of Limitations of James I provided that an owner's right of entry which had not been asserted within twenty years after the right had accrued should be barred. Since the plaintiff in an action of ejectment had the burden of proving that he had at least a right of entry, the fact that the right of entry was thus barred meant that the right to the action of ejectment was really lost after the twenty years had expired.

Sec. 237. Change in the Nature of Statutes of Limitations. Throughout the Middle Ages, only the lack of evidence had constituted a limitation on the writ of right. All of the early statutes of limitation had fixed a point back of which the plaintiff was not allowed to go for a source of title, the limitation dating from the seisin, rather than from the disseisin. The same thing was true of the Statute of Limitations enacted during the reign of Henry VIII, but in the Statute of Limitations of James I, a new method, the modern one, was adopted, that of limiting the right of entry to within a certain period after the accrual of the right, the limitation thus dating from the disseisin.

Sec. 238. Statute of Limitations of James I—Disabilities. The statute of James I contained provisions for extending the time for bringing the action in certain cases where the person entitled was under a disability. Exceptions were thus made in favor of minors under the age of 21, married women, persons *non compos mentis,* persons who were imprisoned and persons who were beyond the seas.

Sec. 239. Statutes of Limitation in the United States. In the United States, all jurisdictions have general statutes of limitation, which however vary in form. Many of them are modeled after the statute of James I. The twenty year period has been adopted in a number of the states, while in others the lapse of a longer or shorter period is required to bar the right of action. Some few of the states have statutes which expressly provide that the right or title of the former owner shall be extinguished after the passage of the stated period, but the majority of them merely bar the remedy by ejectment. It is almost invariably held, however, whatever the form taken by the statute, that the effect of the statute is to take away all other remedy and right of the former owner as well as the action of ejectment.

Sec. 240. Adverse Possession in the United States.[4] The doctrine of adverse possession has been developed in the United States, that long continued possession of land by one other than the true owner, who claims to hold the land as owner, gives rise to the presumption of a valid conveyance either to the holder or to the person under whom he holds. That involves a presumption of the rightfulness of the possession, while the statutes of limitation apply where, apart from such statutes, the possession would be wrongful.

According to the common law ideas of seisin, the true owner did not lose seisin simply by leaving the land and allowing it to remain unoccupied. Nor did the disseisor lose

---

[4] Bordwell, Disseisin and Adverse Possession, (1923) 33 Yale L.J. pp. 1-13, 141-158, 285-301.

his tortious seisin by leaving the land, thus automatically restoring the seisin of the rightful owner. In order to regain seisin, the disseisee had to re-enter the land or make continual claim. In the United States, in the case of adverse possession, no such re-entry or claim was necessary. The doctrine early developed that, unless the land was actually in the adverse possession of one other than the true owner, the title drew possession to itself. That meant that if a gap occurred in adverse holdings, the effect was to start the statute running afresh, since immediately upon the occurrence of the gap, the seisin followed the title.

Under both Henry VIII's and James I's Statutes of Limitation the burden of proving seisin within the statutory period was placed upon the disseisee. The question was not made to turn upon the merits or demerits of the one in possession of the land, but on whether the seisin of the true owner had existed during the requisite period. Since that was the fundamental issue, it did not matter whether the true owner had been kept out of possession by a single disseisor or by a succession of disseisors. In the United States the doctrine of adverse possession was essentially opposed to disseisin in being affirmative in nature. It was an affirmative doctrine in that it was a doctrine of inchoate ownership ripening into ownership with the aid of the statute. The burden of the statute was removed from the true owner and placed upon the claimant, due to the principle that the possession followed the title, until an adverse possession had been clearly made out. In this country, then, the emphasis was laid on the man in possession rather than on the man out of possession.

It is in connection with the doctrine of tacking successive adverse possessions in order to make up the statutory period that the American doctrine of adverse possession is put to the test as a doctrine of affirmative prescription. If the prescription is negative, the primary question is as to the destruction of the old title, rather than the creation of the new. If the extinguishment of the old title is the first question, it may well be enough that possession has been lost for the statutory period, regardless of whether or not throughout that entire period the land has been held by a single adverse possessor, or by a series of adverse possessors all holding under the same claim. On the other hand, if the question first to be considered is whether a new title has been created it will be required that the adverse possessors all hold under the same claim, and there will have to be privity of estate between successive adverse possessors before tacking will be allowed. The American doctrine of adverse possession does meet that test of affirmative prescription.

Sec. 241. **Adverse Possession in the United States—Doctrine that Possession Follows the Title, in the Absence of Proof of Adverse Possession.** The fact that there was an abundance of vacant land in the United States, and there was a multiplicity of disputes over title, led the courts to look with favor upon the regular title, irrespective of whether or not the title holder was actually in possession of the land. In order to accomplish their result, the courts emphasized and rationalized the character in which or the intention with which the land was held. Every presumption in favor of the true owner was indulged, the prevailing doctrine being that until adverse possession had been clearly established, possession followed the title. The doctrine developed early in the courts of New York that possession was presumed to be in subordination to the true title, and the burden of proving possession to be adverse was placed on the claimant, had a very great influence upon the other jurisdictions. New York enacted those principles into its statutes of 1828, and other states followed that example. In many of the remaining jurisdictions, the New York view was regarded as controlling, with the result that with rare exceptions the presumption that possession is not adverse but in subordination to the true title, has been accepted in the United States.

Sec. 242. **Adverse Possession in the United States—Doctrine of "Color of Title."** In general it may be said that a person can acquire by adverse possession only the land that he is actually occupying. There is, however, one important exception to this statement. Where a person is holding land adversely to the true owner, under what is spoken of as "color of title" that is, where he is claiming under an instrument that purports to be a valid muniment of title, he is regarded as being in constructive possession of the whole tract of land conveyed by that instrument, even though he may be occupying only a part of the tract. In many of the western jurisdictions, there is, in addition to the general statute of limitations, a statute fixing a shorter period where land is held under color of title.

Sec. 243. Statutory Provisions in the United States Concerning Persons under Disability. As to the exceptions in the Statute of Limitations of James I, in favor of persons under disabilities, the one in favor of minors has been retained in most states, although the age at which an infant attains majority varies; the one in favor of *femes covert* is still found in some states, although in others it has been expressly abolished in view of the statutory provision affecting the rights of married women to sue alone; in many states the one in favor of persons *non compos mentis,* and the one in favor of those beyond the seas, or the expression that means the same thing with us, absent from the United States, exist. In some states there is an additional exception in favor of alien enemies.

Sec. 244. Adverse Possession in the United States—Conveyances of Land Held Adversely.[5] Transfer of land held adversely has usually been considered to be associated with adverse possession in the United States rather than with seisin and disseisin. The result is that there is not much to be found concerning the alienability of the right of entry, but a great deal concerning the alienability of land in the adverse possession of another. In all but two states there has been some pronouncement on this subject, either by legislation or by decision. From the first, such lands were held to be alienable in twenty-six states; alienability has been established

---

[5] Bordwell, Seisin and Disseisin, (1921) 34 Harv. L. Rev. 734.

in many of the others by statute. The rule of non-transfer-ability is still in force in only seven states.

BIBLIOGRAPHY

Digby, Kenelm Edward, An Introduction to the History of the Law of Real Property (5th ed. 1897), 70-76, 108-115.

Holdsworth, W. S., An Historical Introduction to the Land Law (1927), 10-16, 121-131, 167-175, 177-188.

Holdsworth, W. S., A History of English Law (3d ed. 1931), Vol. III, 1-29, 88-101; Vol. IV, 483-486; Vol. VII, 3-78.

Maitland, The Forms of Action at Common Law (Chaytor and Whittaker ed. 1936), 21-48, 52-60.

Pollock and Maitland, The History of English Law Before the Time of Edward I (2d ed. 1911), Vol. II, 29-79.

Tiffany, The Law of Real Property (2d ed. 1929), Vol. II, secs. 509, 512.

Chapter IV

INCORPOREAL INTERESTS

Sec. 245. Nature of Incorporeal Interests. Blackstone, in the course of his discussion of corporeal and incorporeal hereditaments, declares:

> "But an hereditament, says Sir Edward Coke, is by much the largest and most comprehensive expression; for it includes not only lands and tenements, but whatsoever *may be inherited,* be it corporeal or incorporeal, real, personal, or mixed . . ." [1]

> "Hereditaments, then, to use the largest expression, are of two kinds, corporeal and incorporeal. Corporeal consist of such as affect the senses, such as may be seen and handled by the body; incorporeal are not the objects of sensation, can neither be seen or handled; are creatures of the mind, and exist only in contemplation . . ." [2]

> "An incorporeal hereditament is a right issuing out of a thing corporeal (whether real or personal), or concerning, or annexed to, or exercisable within the same . . ." [3]

Wesley Newcomb Hohfeld makes the following lucid comment on Blackstone's statements:

> "Since all legal interests are 'incorporeal'—consisting, as they do, of more or less limited aggregates of

---

[1] 2 Bl. Comm. c. II * 17.
[2] 2 Bl. Comm. c. II * 17.
[3] 2 Bl. Comm. c. II * 20.

174

abstract legal relations—such a supposed contrast as that sought to be drawn by Blackstone can but serve to mislead the unwary. The legal interest of the fee simple owner of land and the comparatively limited interest of the owner of a 'right of way' over such land are alike so far as 'incorporeality' is concerned; the true contrast consists, of course, primarily in the fact that the fee simple owner's aggregate of legal relations is far more extensive than the aggregate of the easement owner." [4]

Sec. 246. Incorporeal Hereditaments at Common Law— The Ten Incorporeal Hereditaments Listed by Blackstone. Blackstone enumerated ten incorporeal hereditaments: advowsons, tithes, commons, ways, offices, dignities, franchises, corodies, annuities, and rents. Of these, the only ones which have retained any except a purely historical interest for our purposes are commons, ways, and rents.

A. INCORPOREAL HEREDITAMENTS IMPORTANT ONLY AT COMMON LAW

Sec. 247. Creation of Those Incorporeal Hereditaments Which Were Important Only at Common Law. In creating the following seven incorporeal hereditaments, since no possessory interest passed from the grantor to the grantee, despite the durability of the interest being transferred, the only type of conveyance available was the deed of grant. It will be recalled that this was also the type of conveyance used to convey a future interest to a person having no interest in the property, and consisted merely of a sealed writing stating the interest granted.

Sec. 248. Definition of the Incorporeal Hereditaments Which Were Important Only at Common Law. The first of the incorporeal hereditaments listed by Blackstone was an advowson. An advowson was the right of presentation of an

---

[4] Hohfeld, Fundamental Legal Conceptions (1923), 29, 30.

incumbent to a church or ecclesiastical benefice, the right to name the incumbent of a vacant church. During the thirteenth century, advowsons were looked upon as normally being appendant, that is, attached to some particular manor. In general, when the manor was conveyed by feoffment, the advowson also was conveyed as being appendant to the manor. However, an advowson was frequently detached from the manor. The lord might convey the manor, retaining the advowson, or he might convey the advowson, retaining the manor. When an advowson had been separated from the manor, it was thereafter spoken of as an advowson "in gross." Advowsons were protected by the real actions. The proprietary action that was available for the recovery of an advowson was the writ of advowson. The possessory remedy available was the assize of *darrein presentment*.

The second incorporeal hereditament on Blackstone's list was the tithe. A tithe was the tenth part of the yearly increase from the profits of land, stock on the land, and the personal industry of the inhabitants of the parish, payable to the parish parson. The parson's right to tithes was established by statutory law.

Dignities were titles, such as those of the nobility. Franchises were a royal privilege, or branch of the king's prerogative, subsisting in the hands of a subject.

Corodies were the right to receive certain allotments of victuals and provision for one's maintenance. They usually took the form of grants made by a religious house to some person of food, clothing and lodging for a certain period, in consideration of some benefit conferred. In 1285 the right to bring an assize of *novel disseisin* was given to those who had a right of corody.

If a person promised another to pay him a certain amount of money annually, but did not charge the payment of that amount upon any land, an annuity was created. The real actions could not be used for the protection of annuities, but towards the end of the reign of Henry III, protection was extended in the form of a writ of annuity.

Offices were the right to exercise a public or private employment, and to take the fees and emoluments pertaining thereto, whether public, as in the case of magistrates, or private, as in the case of bailiffs and receivers. As early as 1285 certain offices were given the protection of the assize of *novel disseisin*.

All of these incorporeal interests descended to the heir of the holder upon his death, with the exception of tithes, which of course passed not to the parson's heir, but to his successor in office. It would seem that these rights were not devisable.

The seven incorporeal interests above discussed do not exist in the United States, due to the fact that conditions in this country differ from those that obtained in England during the Middle Ages. Neither advowsons, tithes nor dignities could exist in the United States, since we have never had an established church or a nobility. Corodies appear to be obsolete here. Offices have never been granted for longer than the life of the grantee. Franchises do exist here, but have lost all connection with realty. The most common are corporate franchises and public utility franchises. Strictly speaking, they have no connection with the common law franchise. Annuities also are found in the United States, but have little importance for us, since they are more frequently contractual than real.

B. INCORPOREAL HEREDITAMENTS IMPORTANT AT MODERN LAW

Sec. 249. Changes in Terminology. A change in terminology should be noted in regard to two of the remaining incorporeal interests listed by Blackstone. Today commons are known both as commons and profits, while ways are spoken of both as ways and easements. Rents have undergone no change in terminology.

Sec. 250. Nature of Commons at Common Law. At common law, common or a right of common was a privilege which one had in another's land for a specified purpose. In considering rights of common at common law, we must remember

that for centuries the lands of England were cultivated under
the open field system, which of course meant that rights of
common were of considerable importance. Such rights were
numerous. Among them were: the common of turbary, or the
right to cut turf or fuel, the common of estovers, or the right
to cut timber for fuel, the common of piscary, or the right
to fish, and most important, the common of pasture.

Sec. 251. Common of Pasture at Common Law—Varieties.
The rights of common of pasture were classified as common
appendant, common appurtenant, common in gross, common
pur cause de vicinage and common of shack. Common appendant was the right of common given by law to all the freehold tenants of a manor to pasture on the waste lands of the
manor their commonable beasts *lévant et couchant,* if their
tenement constituted a part of the arable land of the manor.
Cattle *lévant et couchant* were those beasts which manured
the land. Common appendant was always an incident attaching to a certain tract of land, and the right was spoken of as
being vested in the land itself, such land being called the dominant tenement. Common appurtenant, on the other hand,
was not an incident of the tenure of land, and was unlike
common appendant in that, instead of being given by operation of law to all the freehold tenants of the manor, it depended on express grant or prescription, and so might be
given to one not a tenant of the manor, might be enjoyed in
respect to land not a part of the ancient arable land of the
manor, and might exist as to other than commonable cattle.
Common appendant and common appurtenant were alike,
however, in that both were rights annexed to the ownership
of a dominant tenement, and therefore in both the extent of
the right was limited by the needs of the dominant tenement.
Common in gross was not annexed to the ownership of any
particular land, but was a personal right of the holder. Common *pur cause de vicinage* existed where the tenants of two
different manors that had adjoining waste lands were allowed
to pasture their cattle on the wastes of the other manor.
Common of shack existed in certain localities, and was the

right at certain times of the year, as after harvest but before the sowing of crops, to pasture cattle on the fields, or to pasture cattle on the field that was being allowed to lie fallow. These rights were not restricted to freehold tenants but were extended to the villein holders and copyholders as well.

Sec. 252. Common of Pasture at Common Law—Effect of the Enclosure Movement. During the thirteenth century, the lords wanted to bring their waste lands under cultivation and the problem therefore arose as to how far they could by so doing interfere with the rights of common. The Statute of Merton and the Statute of Westminster II which were enacted during the course of that century, allowed improvement of the waste lands so long as a sufficiency of common was left to the commoners. These statutes were restricted in their application to common appendant and to common *pur cause de vicinage*. The later statutes which provided for the enclosure of common fields also provided for the partition and enclosure of lands over which rights of common existed.

Sec. 253. Decline of Common Appendant, Common of Shack and Common Pur Cause de Vicinage. Commons appurtenant increased while the other types decreased. The Statute of Quia Emptores of 1290 had provided that, on a conveyance in fee simple, the feoffee held the land, not of the feoffor, but of the chief lord. Since then after such a conveyance the tenant no longer held of the lord of the manor, one of the effects of the statute was to decrease the number of cases in which common appendant could be claimed by a freeholder as incident to his tenure of land. As the common field system was abandoned, common of shack ceased to be of importance and common *pur cause de vicinage* was made infrequent by the improvement of the country.

Sec. 254. Nature of Commons—Rise of Profits at Common Law. In addition to the ten incorporeal hereditaments listed by Blackstone, from the time of Bracton, new interests known as servitudes started to appear. One of these servitudes very similar to the common law right of common was known as a profit à prendre. A profit à prendre was the privilege of entering the land of another and either taking a portion of the soil or a portion of the produce of the soil. Bracton borrowed many of his ideas concerning servitudes from the Roman law. A profit à prendre was recoverable by the assize of *novel disseisin.*

Sec. 255. Nature of Ways—Rise of Easements at Common Law. Blackstone defined ways as the right of going over another man's land. Ways were later known as easements, one of the servitudes mentioned by Bracton, who went to the Roman law for many of his ideas on the subject. Coke later copied some of those ideas that Bracton had borrowed. Even so late as the nineteenth century, the nature of an easement was a doubtful quantity. According to modern law, an easement is either the privilege of using the land of another for certain defined purposes or of preventing the owner of such land from using his land in certain defined ways. In the first case, where the privilege of the owner of the dominant tenement is to do certain positive acts, the easement is called a positive easement; in the second case, where the privilege of the owner of the dominant tenement is simply to prevent acts from being done which will interfere with the enjoyment of his property, the easement is called a negative easement. In both cases, the duty of the owner of the servient tenement is to permit. An easement, like a profit à prendre, is a right which is in addition to the natural rights incident to ownership. In the time of Bracton, it was not settled whether there could be an easement in gross; later it was clear that there could not be. In his time, however, it was established that such privileges could be acquired either by grant or by prescription. Like natural rights, easements were protected by proceedings for nuisance, originally by the assize of nuisance, later by an action on the case for nuisance.

Sec. 256. Nature of Rents at Common Law. Blackstone defines a rent as a certain sum issuing yearly out of the lands and tenements corporeal. The word was derived from the Latin *"redditus."* Rent was regarded as a real thing, issuing out of the land, and was recoverable by the assize of *novel* *disseisin.* There were three kinds of rents, rent service, rent *seck* and rent charge.

A. Rent service was the service (afterwards commuted into a money rent) due as an incident of the tenure. For an arrearage in rent service, the lord had the remedy of distraint which has already been discussed. Since rent was regarded as akin to realty, the holder of the rent could grant it to a third person.

B. Rent *seck* was a rent service which had been granted to a third person by the original holder of the rent. After the conveyance, the remedy of distraint, really a form of self-help, was destroyed and was not available to the grantee of the rent. Hence, this rent was a "dry" or *seck* rent.

C. Rent charge was a rent in which the lord was expressly given the power of distraint by agreement between the parties. The Statute of Quia Emptores had the effect of making a reservation of rent service upon a grant in fee simple impossible. The same result was reached by the grantee's charging the land with the payment of the rent to the grantor and expressly giving him the power of distraint.

Sec. 257. Rights of Commons—Profits in the United States. Rights of profit exist in the United States and are sometimes called commons. They are very important since they are the basis of our mining law. Common appendant cannot exist in this country, nor have we ever had common *pur cause de vicinage.* We do, however, have rights of common appurtenant and common in gross, which are the rights of pasture annexed to a dominant tenement or belonging to a person and his heirs.

Sec. 258. Rights of Way—Easements in the United States. Rights of way exist in the United States, and are treated as easements. They are of great importance.

Sec. 259. Rents in the United States. Rents charge occur but seldom in the United States. Even at the present time, since the Statute of Quia Emptores did not apply to a conveyance in less than fee simple, a rent service is created by the reservation of rent upon the conveyance or lease by a tenant in fee of a lessor estate. The rent reserved in the ordinary lease for years is properly speaking a rent service.

Sec. 260. Acquisition of Incorporeal Interests at Common Law. We have not yet considered the method of acquisition of rights of common, ways, and rents at common law. The right of common appendant was one that was incident to the tenure of land, and was given by operation of law. Common *pur cause de vicinage* was merely a permissive privilege; that is, the existence of the privilege meant that a person could do acts on another's lands which would otherwise have constituted an actionable trespass. Rents were created by a deed of grant. Rights of common appurtenant, common in gross, ways, and servitudes, that is, easements and profits à prendre, could be gained either by deed of grant or by prescription.

Sec. 261. Prescription as a Method of Acquisition of Incorporeal Interests at Common Law. Prescription or long-continued user was a method by which certain incorporeal interests could be acquired at common law. Rights in gross or rights appendant or appurtenant could be established by the claimant's showing that he and all of his predecessors in title had enjoyed those rights from before the time of legal memory. The time of legal memory was fixed at 1189. It was felt during the twelfth and thirteenth centuries that a grantor who gave such a right to his grantee was subjecting his land to a special law, that is, to a law to which it would not have been liable in the absence of such a grant. When the right was questioned, the person claiming it had three ways open to him of establishing his claim. He could either produce the deed of grant which had created the special law in his favor, or he could show that he had enjoyed the right from time immemorial, or he could show that in the place where the land lay, all those situated as he was, enjoyed such a right.

It was only things that were "against the common right" that could be prescribed for, e.g., common appurtenant or servitudes, that is, profits à prendre and easements. By the end of the mediaeval period, a change had taken place in the idea as to the basis of prescription. Since things that could be acquired by prescription as being "against common right" were normally created by a deed of grant, it came to be thought that the basis of prescription was that the fact of immemorial user was conclusive evidence of a grant which had been made before the time of legal memory, rather than that the basis was a special law in favor of the grantee. At that time, the main characteristics of prescription as a method of acquisition of incorporeal interests were clear. Prescription was a means of acquiring certain incorporeal rights over land by a user, which user must have been open and as of right, and have been enjoyed from the time of legal memory. Unless the right were such as could be granted, it could not be acquired through prescription. The user was effective in supplying the place of a lost grant.

The requirement of user from before the time of legal memory, that is, from before 1189, placed a very great burden upon a claimant. The courts therefore held that proof of enjoyment so far back as living witnesses could testify to from their recollection raised a presumption of enjoyment since before 1189, but that presumption was capable of being rebutted. Later the courts in their effort to alleviate the hardship on claimants held that a deed granting the title to the incorporeal interest would be presumed after a certain period of time had elapsed, which period, by analogy to the Statute of Limitations for real actions, was placed at twenty years. Until the end of the eighteenth century, however, this presumption of a grant after user that had lasted for twenty years was rebuttable. In 1832 a statute was passed which provided that exercise and enjoyment of an easement or profit for certain fixed periods had the effect of creating an indefeasible title to the right in question.

Sec. 262. Acquisition of Incorporeal Interests in the United States by Grant. Such incorporeal interests as exist in the United States can be created by deed of grant.

Sec. 263. Acquisition of Incorporeal Interests in the United States by Prescription. In this country, in general, the courts have followed the analogy of the Statutes of Limitations for real property, and have held that where a person has exercised, as of right, a user for the period fixed by the statute, he has acquired a right of user to that extent. Although fairly often the statement is made that a grant will be presumed from the fact of such user, the presumption is not rebuttable, but is in effect a rule of law, with the result that evidence that no such grant had in fact been made would be immaterial but evidence of incapacity so that no such grant could have been made will rebut the presumption.

Sec. 264. Conveyance of Incorporeal Interests at Common Law and in the United States. It is, of course, obvious that incorporeal interests were not capable of physical control and so could not be conveyed by feoffment with livery of seisin. Deeds of grant, by the close of the mediaeval period, had come to be the usual method of transferring incorporeal interests. However, it is notable that even in the case of such incorporeals, something comparable to seisin was required, since the grantee was not accorded full protection until he could show some actual user of the right. There has been no appreciable change in the United States in the method of transferring incorporeal interests.

It should be noted that upon alienation of the land, the incorporeal interests appurtenant thereto pass with the land.

Sec. 265. Devolution on Death of Incorporeal Interests at Common Law and in the United States. As to devolution on death, all of the incorporeal interests when appendant or appurtenant to the land passed at the death of the holder of the land to his heir or devisee. All incorporeal interests in gross terminated on the death of the holder thereof, with the result that there was nothing to be disposed of after his death.

BIBLIOGRAPHY

Ballantine, Title by Adverse Possession, (1919) 32 Harv. L. Rev. 135.
2 Bl. Comm. * 21-43.
Bordwell, Seisin and Disseisin, (1921) 34 Harv. L. Rev. 592.
Digby, Introduction to the History of the Law of Real Property (5th ed. 1897), 181-210, 231-233.

Holdsworth, An Historical Introduction to the Land Law (1927), 89-102, 265-288.

Holdsworth, A History of the English Law (3d ed. 1931), Vol. III, 137-157, 166-171; Vol. VII, 312-350.

Pollock and Maitland, The History of English Law Before the Time of Edward I (2d ed. 1911), 123-148.

Taylor, Titles to Land by Adverse Possession, (1934) 20 Iowa L. Rev. 738.

Tiffany, The Law of Real Property (2d ed. 1929), Vol. II, 1257-1327, 1388-1400.

CHAPTER V

ESTATES HELD IN CO-OWNERSHIP

Sec. 266. Co-ownership—Varieties at Common Law. During the fifteenth century, four kinds of estates held in co-ownership, as opposed to several ownership, or ownership by one person alone, were recognized: joint tenancy, coparcenary, tenancy by the entireties and tenancy in common. In all these types of co-ownership, the co-owners had simultaneously interests in every portion of the land, but no separate interest in any one portion of the land. They were interested, according to the extent of their share, in every part of the land.

Sec. 267. Joint Tenancy at Common Law. The estate of the joint tenant was marked by four unities: unity of title, time, interest, and possession. It was necessary to constitute an estate so held that the joint tenants get the estate by the same title, that they begin to enjoy it at the same time, that they take the same interest, and have the same possession. Until the reign of Henry VIII, a joint tenant had to obtain the consent of all the other tenants before he could partition. If he wished to convey his interest to one of the other joint tenants, it was necessary for him to use a release, since he was seised of the whole land. In the event of the death of a joint tenant, the other joint tenants took his interest by survivorship. Any grant to two persons was construed to be a joint tenancy.

Sec. 268. Coparcenary at Common Law. Coparcenary

existed where several persons took as co-heirs. In the event that the holder of an estate in fee simple died, leaving only daughters, under the common law rules of descent, the daughters took as co-heiresses in coparcenary. In an estate so held, there were three unities: unity of title, interest, and possession. It was possible for one of the coparceners to compel partition by writ of partition. One coparcener could convey her interest to the others by feoffment with livery of seisin or by release. There was no right of survivorship; the interest of a coparcener descended to her heirs on her death.

Sec. 269. Tenancy by the Entireties at Common Law. Tenancy by the entireties could exist at common law only where an estate was given to a husband and wife, whom the law regarded as one person. There was only unity of possession in an estate so held. Survivorship was an incident of this tenancy. Where an estate had been given in that fashion, unless the husband conveyed it by fine, it had to come to the wife on his death, regardless of any alienation he had made, or any forfeiture he had incurred.

Sec. 270. Tenancy in Common at Common Law. Tenancy in common occurred where the tenants held by several and distinct titles, but still had unity of possession. At early common law, it was not possible for a tenant in common to compel partition, but this was changed by legislation enacted during the reigns of Henry VIII and William III. There was no right of survivorship where an estate was so held.

Sec. 271. Development of Estates of Co-ownership at Common Law. During the time of Bracton, about the middle of the thirteenth century, coparcenary, joint tenancy, and perhaps tenancy by the entireties were already recognized. At that period it was settled that survivorship attached to joint tenancy. In 1340 it was settled that survivorship did not attach to the interest of a coparcener. As early as the time of Bracton, the distinction between the estate of the joint tenant and that of the coparcener as to partition had been established; it was clear that each coparcener had the right to the writ of partition, whereas in the case of joint tenants, one joint tenant could not partition without first obtaining the consent of the other tenants. By the time of Edward I, the distinction between joint tenancy and tenancy in common was becoming fixed.

Sec. 272. **Joint Tenancy, Coparcenary, Tenancy by the Entireties and Tenancy in Common in the United States.** In many jurisdictions of the United States, there is a statutory provision to the effect that a conveyance or devise to two or more persons shall create not a joint tenancy, but a tenancy in common, in the absence of a contrary intent clearly appearing. Sometimes the statute provides that the contrary intent must be clearly expressed. Joint tenancy has also been expressly abolished by statute in some states, where the statute provides that what would have created a joint tenancy at common law shall create a tenancy in common. In some jurisdictions, statutes have expressly abolished the incident of survivorship in a joint tenancy. Instances of coparcenary are infrequent in this country. Whether or not there is a statute so providing, land that descends to two or more persons is usually considered as creating a tenancy in common. The interest of the coparcener, however, is still recognized in some states. So far as tenancy by the entireties is concerned, the statutes providing that a grant to two or more persons shall in the absence of the expression of a contrary intent create a tenancy in common have usually been construed to have no application to tenancy by the entireties, although the opposite result has also been reached. The same thing is true of the Married Women's Property Acts. In some few jurisdictions, even in the absence of legislation, tenancy by the entireties has been repudiated as being out of line with the modern conception of the marital relationship.

Sec. 273. **Community Property in the United States.** A type of co-ownership that exists in several of the southern and western states, which did not exist at common law, must be mentioned. In Louisiana, Texas, California, Arizona, Idaho, New Mexico, Nevada, and Washington, a system known as the community property system prevails; whatever is acquired after marriage by the efforts of either the husband or the wife constitutes community property belonging equally to the spouses. It is, however, possible for either the husband or wife, or both, to have in addition, property other than community, which is termed separate property. Separate property is usually defined by statute as being property belonging to either at the time of the marriage, and also property acquired after the marriage by gift, devise or descent or in exchange for separate property. Separate property also includes the rents, issues, and profits of separate property, except in Texas, Louisiana, and Idaho. In each of the states which have adopted the community property system, there is either an express or implied statutory provision that all property which is not separate property is community property. Property acquired by either the husband or wife after the marriage is presumed to be community property, until it is shown to be separate. The sole control over the community property is usually vested in the husband. In Louisiana and Texas, on the death of the wife, the husband has the control of the community property for the purpose of settling the community affairs. In three states, California, Nevada, and Idaho, on the death of the wife, the husband becomes absolute owner of all the community property. In the other states, the half belonging to either spouse descends to his or her heirs subject to payment of debts. Of course, it is possible for the devolution to be controlled by will. In the event that there are no heirs and no will, in some jurisdictions the surviving spouse takes the interest held by the deceased. It is obvious that where the community property system prevails, rights of dower and curtesy cannot exist.

Sec. 274. Conveyance of Interest of Co-owner. As to the transfer of the interest of a co-owner, mention has already been made of partition, which alone need be considered. Partition was in general effected by deed and such a deed was required in the case of joint tenants and tenants in common. The Statute of Frauds of course made a deed necessary in all cases.

Sec. 275. Devolution on Death of the Interest of Co-owner. The only interests held by co-owners that could descend upon the death of the holder were those interests to which the right of survivorship did not attach and the same thing was true as to devisability.

BIBLIOGRAPHY

Holdsworth, W. S., An Historical Introduction to the Land Law (1927), 69-70.

Tiffany, The Law of Real Property (2d ed. 1929), Vol. I, secs. 190, 191, 192-195.

INDEX

(References are to section numbers.)

—A—

(References are to section numbers.)

(References are to section numbers.)

(References are to section numbers.)

(References are to section numbers.)

(References are to section numbers.)

—L—

—M—

—N—

—O—

(References are to section numbers.)

—P—

Paravail, Tenant, 4

Particular Estate, 162, 170-173, 182, 185, 188, 190, 191, 193, 194

Partition, 267-271, 274

Pasture, Common of, 250

Pennsylvania, Tenure in, 46

Periodic Tenancy, 139, 140, 141

Petit Serjeanty, 15

Piscary, Common of, 250

Possession, 217
    See also *Adverse Possession*

Possessory Actions, 220, 221, 248

Possibility of Reverter, 83, 86, 87, 157-161
    Possibility of Reverter, Creation in Third Person, 158, 159
    Possibility of Reverter, Devisability of, 160, 161
    Possibility of Reverter, Devolution of, 160, 161
    Possibility of Reverter, Transfer of, 158, 159

Powers of Appointment, 213-215

Powers of Termination, 84, 86, 87, 123

Praecipe in Capite, 219

Preceding Estate, 170-173, 182-185, 188, 190, 191, 193, 194

Prescription, 255, 260, 261, 263

Presumptive Heir, 52

Primer Seisin, 10

Primogeniture, 75, 76

Profits, 249, 254, 257, 260, 261

Proprietary Actions, 219

Pur Autre Vie, Estate, 109, 115, 118, 119

Pur Cause de Vicinage, Common, 250, 251, 253, 257, 26ʟ

Purchase, 52, 186

—Q—

Qualified Fee Simple, 82-87

Quare Clausum Fregit, 124, 130, 135

Quare Ejecit Infra Terminum, 124, 130, 135

(References are to section numbers.)

—T—

(References are to section numbers.)

—U—

(References are to section numbers.)

—W—

—Y—

www.ingramcontent.com/pod-product-compliance
Lightning Source LLC
Chambersburg PA
CBHW021556210326
41599CB00010B/462